Who Killed Jesse James
New Clues To The Old Mystery

By Western Historian and Author
Dr. Roy William Roush, Ph.D.

Published by Front Line Press

Copyright August 2011
ISBN: 0-9723072-8-1

First Edition
Proudly Printed in The United States of America

Copies of this or the other books can be ordered from Front Line Press
5150 Escobedo, Woodland Hills, CA 91364
(818) 888-5416
Or from the Website: knightsofthegoldencircle.net

All rights reserved. No part of this book may be used, reproduced, photocopied, stored in any retrieval system, recorded, or transmitted by any means whatsoever without written permission from the author or publisher (except for brief quotes, reviews, references, or excerpts, provided proper credit is given.)

Credits of Dr. Roush

BA Degree in Journalism from Oklahoma State University in 1950; plus a MA and Ph.D in Biblical Archaeology, St. Charles University in 1999.

Author of five recent books:
  Jesse James and Lost Treasures of the Knights of The Golden Circle
  The Mysterious and Secret Order of the Knights of The Golden Circle
  Knights of The Golden Circle Treasure Signs
  How To Find The Treasures of The Knights of The Golden Circle
  Lost Treasure Secrets

For many years was a columnist, feature story writer and staff member on the following publications: Treasure; Treasure Search; Treasure Found; Treasure Diver; Treasure Hunter; and the Treasure News. Also, was the editor and feature story writer for The Treasure Hunter Confidential Newsletter; Biblical and American Archeologist and The Adventures' Club News of Los Angeles. Previously had been a writer for The Kansas City Star; Rocky Mountain Aviation Magazine and The Las Vegas Magazine.

Also, author of the prize-winning book "Open Fire" a 707-page story of the author's combat experience in WWII with the 2nd Marine Division during the four epic battles of Guadalcanal, Tarawa, Saipan and Tinian in the South Pacific against the Japanese. Plus, his four years experience as an Air Force P-51 and Jet Fighter Pilot during the Korean War. The book was awarded the "Best Non-Fiction Book of 2004" by the Book Publicists of Southern California and has been described as the best personal experience of combat in WWII. Author is also a popular speaker around the country about his experiences to clubs and organizations, and also on radio and TV.

Appeared in two of the best selling video games on WWII by Electronic Arts Entertainment: Medal of Honor--The Rising Sun and The Assault on Tarawa to describe and explain the combat scenes and the Banzi attacks being shown.

Recently appeared as a consultant on History Channel's two-hour documentary special: Jesse James' Hidden Treasure.

Also, was chosen to be the consultant for the prominently featured 2008 Walt Disney Movie, National Treasure II, Book of Secrets, staring Nicolas Cage and produced by Walt Disney/Jerry Bruckheimer Studios; also interviewed and shown in their Collectors DVD Edition.

Has worked with and has appeared on various television programs, including: Treasure of Elysian Park on Unsolved Mysteries; several of Bill Burrud's Searching For Lost Treasures; NBC's Special Series on Diving For Spanish Treasure Galleons In Varacruz Mexico; ABC's Series on How to Find Lost Treasure and The Hunt for Amazing Treasures; The Frank Sayer Show on The Lost Dutchman Mine and American

Treasure Hunters; Searching For 17 Tons of Gold, filmed by the Tokyo Broadcasting Company in 1998; Al Capone's Hide-out In Palm Springs with Eye On LA Series; The Loot of Lima, a TV special; Treasure Hunting, a Milas Henshaw Production; then recently was Co-Host on Americas' Lost Treasures Series, plus numerous other television shows and radio broadcasts. Even as a stunt pilot and a dirt bike rider in a feature movie, Bimini Code, a story of hunting for lost treasure.

For many years, taught classes on ghost town, treasure hunting and gold prospecting at UCLA and Los Angeles City College.

Currently, the author can be seen in the best selling and popular DVD, "Prospecting for Gold--The Six Basic Methods of Finding Gold," a professional one-hour video in which the author shows how to find gold bearing areas, then how to choose and operate the equipment best suited to recover it, including techniques for panning, sluicing, wet and dry washing, dredging, metal detecting, etc. The DVD can be purchased at most gold prospecting and treasure hunting shops, or on the Internet.

Author retired from aerospace as a Service Engineer and Technical Writer on Pilots Handbooks and Service Manuals.

References

Information in this book on the life and activities of Jesse James and his gang are based on information in the following books:

1. "The Album Of Gunfighters" by J. Marvin Hunter and Noah H. Rose, published in 1951.

2. "Bill Kelly's Encyclopedia of Gunmen" Collectors Edition, published in 1976, Number 470 of a Limited Edition of 500, autographed to myself by the author in 1986.

3. "Guns and the Gunfighters" by the editors of Guns & Ammo, first published in 1975.

4. "The Gunfighters" by the Editors of Time-Life Books, published in 1974.

5. "The Gunfighters" by Dale T. Schoenberger, published in 1982.

6. "Oklahoma Treasures and Treasure Tales" by Steve Wilson, published in 1976.

7. "The Outlaws" by James D. Horan. Horan is considered one of the premier biographers on the life of Jesse James and his gang, published in 1997.

8. "The Outlaw Trail" by Robert Redford, published in 1978.

9. "Pictorial History of the Wild West" by James D. Horan and Paul Sann, published in 1954.

10. "Historical Atlas of the Outlaw West" by Richard Patterson, published in 1985.

11. "Saga of Jesse James" by Carl W. Breihan. He is also recognized as one of the best biographers of Jesse James. It was published in 1991.

Note: All of these books have been in my personal library for a number of years, and have been reviewed for the purpose of writing this book, especially the books by Breihan and Horan that contain a lot of detailed information on the life and activities of Jesse James.

Though the conventional view at the time when these books were written, it was thought that Bob Ford had killed Jesse James; however it was brought out that there were still many doubts and suspicions among the public from some people who knew Jesse. They said that since he had tried a hoax one time before, he might be trying it again.

The writers also commented on the events following the shooting as being strange and unusual. These books were all written long before the body that was buried in Jesse's grave was exhumed in 1995 for DNA testing that revealed evidence it didn't match with some people who said they were relatives of Jesses'. Most of the authors also questioned the old theory that Jesse was killed, and who was buried instead of Jesse!

Though, there has been much information on the internet and in magazines on Jesse's life and his death that gives many different versions, I have deferred from all of them because they may or may not be reliable.

CONTENTS

Front Matter
   Title Page
   Credits of The Author
   References
   Introduction

Chapt. 1. JESSE JAMES 1
   Most Wanted Man 1
    Was Loved or Hated 2
    The KGC 3
    Born in Missouri in 1847 3
    Civil War Solder 4
    Turned Bandit 5
    Man of Many Traits 5
     Physically And Mentally Tough 6
     A Hunted Man 6
    Reward Posters 7
     His Gang 7
     Gads Hill Trail Robbery 8
     John Wesley Hardin 8
     Very Secretive 9
   Well Armed 10
    America's Robin Hood 10
   Members Of The KGC 11
   A Jesse James Treasure Found 12
   Jesse's Secret Life 12
    The Appeal of Bandit Life 12
    KGC In History 13

Chapt. 2. THE BIG NORTHFIELD BANK ROBBERY AND SHOOTOUT 18
   Things Go Wrong 19
   Big Gun Battle 19
   Their Desperate Ride To Escape 19
   Chased By Posses 20
   The Wounded 21
  Jim Younger Seriously Injured 21
   Keeping Ahead Of The Posses 22
   Jesse Demands Bob Younger Be Left Behind 23
  A Possible Gunfight Between Jesse and Cole Younger 23
   Frank And Jesse Escape 24
   End Of The Chase 24
  Model Prisoners 25
  Released From Prison 26

I

Chapt. 3. BOB FORD CLAIMES HE KILLED JESSE JAMES..................31
   A National Sensation..................31
   Was Hard To Believe..................31
     Large Reward..................31
   Few People Knew What Jesse Looked Like..................32
   Jesse's New Gang..................32
   Bob's Strange Stories..................33
    That Morning..................33
   Jesse Takes His Guns Off..................33
    Stood On A Chair..................34
   Bob Sees His Chance..................34
   What Have You Done..................35
   Jesse's Wife Did Not Weep..................35
   Jesse Was Always Alert..................36
   Fast On The Draw..................36
    Questions And Doubts..................37
   The Mysterious Dead Man..................37
   Who Was Bob Ford..................37
   Body Was Similar..................38
   Governor Declares Jesse Was Killed..................38
   Why The Governor Acted..................38
   The Governor's Campaign Promise..................39
   Jesse And The Governor Were Old Friends..................39
   The Governor's Secret Meeting With The Fords..................40
   Secret Meetings Never Denied..................40
   Body Was Guarded..................41
   Finally Buried..................41
   Bob And Charles Ford Go On Trial For Murder..................41
   Governor Intercedes And Pardons Them..................41
   The Myth..................41
   Should History Be Rewritten..................42
   Events Later..................42
   Bob Ford Murdered..................42
    Charles Ford Said To Have Committed Suicide..................43
   Frank James Surrenders..................43
    Frank's Pardon..................44
   Jesse's Son..................44
   Jesse's Mother..................44

Chapt. 4. THE REST OF THE STORY—EXPOSING THE HOAX..................53
   DNA Evidence..................53
   The Strange Bullet..................54
   Photographic Evidence..................54
   Tintype Photos..................55
   No Photos of Jesse's Body Scars..................55
   The Coroner's Predicament..................56

- The Governor's Connection..57
- Who Was Killed Instead of Jesse...57
- Charlie Bigelow..58
- The Bullet In The Wall...59
- Do The Photos Give Away A Secret..59
  - Jesse's First Hoax Attempt...60
- George Shepherd Claimed He Had Killed Jesse.................................60
- Was A Put-Job...60
- Jesse Was A Clever Person..61
- Many Doubts Reported..61
- Chicago Newspaper Reports Jesse Was Not Killed............................61
- The Reward Money...62
- Jesse's Secret Meeting With The Governor..63
- J. Frank Dalton..64
- The Examination Showed...64
- Some Outlaws Lived With Many Bullet Wounds..............................65
  - Texas Jack..65
  - Strange Photo of Bob Ford..66
- The Read Secret Of Frank and Jesse James..66
  - Bob And Charles Never Hid Out...67
  - Jesse's Epitaph...68
- Afterwards..68
- A Peace Treaty...68

Chapt. Five. THE FORD BROTHERS ON TRIAL..................................72
- False Confessions...72
- The Secret Agreement With The Governor..72
- The Brothers Had Been Lucky..73
- The Hoax..74
- A Quick Change Of Pleas..75
- Defending Themselves..76
- A New Trial...77
- Guilty Or Not...77
- Who Was Killed..78
- A Cousin That Resembled Jesse...78
- The Cousin Who Had Used The Name Of Howard...........................79
- Wood Hite..80
- Living Relatives...81
- Who Would Pay For The Crime...88

About The Author..91

LIST OF ILLUSTRATIONS

Reward Posters For Jesse James...15
Jesse's Mother With Left Arm Missing...16
Newspaper Copy of An Interesting Story..17
The First National Bank Building At Northfield..27
Bodies Of The Three Bandits Killed...28
Three Younger Brothers In Prison..29
Cole Younger...30
Bob And Charles Ford..46
Cartoon of Jesse As An Angle and Of Cole Younger As A Speaker.........................47
Jesse's House...48
Sketch Of Bob Ford Shooting Jesse James...49
Picture Of Man Who Was Killed..50
Picture Of Jesse With A High Hairline...51
Picture Of Governor Crittenden 52
Who's Grave Is This..70
Carefully Posed Picture of Bob Ford With Crossed Fingers.........................73
Newspaper Article That Jesse James Is Alive...83
The Streets Were Crowded With People..84
Jesse James (Alias J. Frank Dalton) At 100-Years Old.................................85
The Affidavit...86
Jesse (Alias J. Frank Dalton) With Famous Oklahoma Outlaw, Al Jenning.................87
Jesse (Alias J. Frank Dalton) With Treasure Hunter Joe Hunter & The Brass Kettle....88
Last Picture Of Frank James..89

INTRODUCTION

With the exception of a few Presidents or politicians, no person in our history has been as famous and as controversial over the years as Jesse James. About half of our country thought he was a patriot and a hero; while at the same time, about half thought he was a bandit and a cold-blooded killer.

Actually, he was both. So, he was either feared or praised, and was either running from the law, or being protected by some in the law, including some politicians and others who sympathized with him.

His life was full of action and violence, but also shrouded in mystery—even to the reports of his death! Was he really killed by Bob Ford in 1882, or was it actually a grand hoax that was staged with someone else being killed and buried in his grave so that Jesse could escape from the law and secretly live on to be an old man as many people believe; and if so, was he involved in a secret mission afterwards to help the Confederates and the KGC?

Jesse and his brother, Frank, had fought on the side of the South during the Civil War as members of Quantrill's Raiders and participated in some of the worst fighting of the war. Then, feeling that society had turned against them, they turned to a life of crime.

For 15 years, he was hunted and chased as a gang leader, but amazingly, never once was he captured or saw the inside of a jail, though there was a very large reward out for him—dead or alive! Jesse was very lucky, but also very clever.

The story of his assassination was sensational, but also quite strange and it was hard to believe Bob Fords version of it. It didn't seem plausible and didn't add up. Also, Bob changed his stories several times. Many people believed that Jesse was still alive and that someone else was killed instead of him.

So the Governor, for reasons of his own, stepped in and claimed that it was Jesse who had been killed. And that's how history has told it. But the doubts and suspicions about it have never gone away.

Then recently, there has been a renewed interests and a re-examination of the events since there has been some new scientific evidence, plus some other convincing information that conflicts with the old story. It supports the conclusion that history has told it wrong and that the public has been deceived for years.

Some people today claim to be descendents of Jesse, and I have met at least three or four of them including one who claimed to be a great-grandson of Jesse and one who claims to be a great-granddaughter, and they all believe that Jesse was not killed by Bob Ford, but lived on to be an old man.

Many historical writers in the past spent too much time rewriting and copying each other's material instead of searching the records themselves. If they had, we could have learned much sooner what really happened!

History should be rewritten—and maybe it is!

Chapter One

JESSE JAMES

The life of Jesse James was truly amazing. It was one of the most colorful and interesting in our history. He became a legend in his own lifetime and still remains one today. Many myths and legends grew up about him. Some were true and some were not. His story is as exciting as any adventure novel. He seemed bigger than life and if anybody ever lived on the razor's edge, it was Jesse James!

His life was full of daring adventures, gunfights, Civil War battles, robberies, controversies, and mysteries--even as to whether he was really killed, or had he staged an elaborated hoax to make it appear that he had been killed so he could escape from the law and live in hiding for years. And if so, did he secretly work with the Knights of The Golden Circle thereafter? There are some good reasons to believe he did. That, plus some other events in his life have been shrouded in mystery leaving many unanswered questions about his life.

Most Wanted Man

He was the most wanted man in our country for over 15 years, and has inspired many stories, books, plays, TV programs, and numerous movies--28 movies at last count, and I just saw a new one. But most were highly fictionalized which have led to a considerable amount of misinformation about him, especially in the movies.

He and his gang were always big news, especially if a shoot-out was involved. It helped to sell a lot of newspapers. Reporters would always flock to wherever his latest robbery had been, and sometimes to ones they didn't commit. It was hard to tell because bandits always wore masks, but sometimes their horses could be identified.

Frequently, other bandits would imitate Jesse's style of robbery when they would suddenly appear with drawn weapons on unsuspecting victims, quickly demanding money, then quickly disappearing. But sometimes, robberies like this would happen just a day or so apart at locations that were too far from each other to have been performed by the same robbers, so Jesse couldn't have been involved in both. But sometimes, robberies were blamed on Jesse and his gang when authorities didn't know who else to blame it on, or when someone posed as Jesse.

Jesse was always irritated when he was blamed for robberies he didn't commit, so he would sometimes write letters of protest to the editors of the Kansas City Star or other newspapers declaring his innocence of the charges against him. They were always well written which attested to Jesse's education and intelligence. The letters were usually published and attracted considerable attention.

He was always a popular subject of public discussion and opinions for many years. I remember hearing my grandfather, on my father's side, who was born in Joplin, Missouri in 1885, occasionally talk about some of the things he had heard about Jesse, as well as some of the other outlaws, including Billy The Kid. When he was a young man, my grandfather had worked in the zinc mines in Missouri and his roommate was a cousin to Billy.

Some of the letters published by the newspapers were from people in support of him for his defiance against the North, while others would write letters or articles expressing their outrage over him and his gang.

To some, especially those who lived in the South, Jesse was considered a hero and a patriot who robbed from the North and gave to the South, while to others, he was considered a vicious criminal, a daring bandit, a cold-blooded killer and public enemy number one.

That was a strange contradiction, but there was some truth to both issues. Sometimes he was praised and sometimes condemned. Sometimes he was hunted by the law and sometimes sheltered by the law, including some public officials.

Was Loved or Hated

Opinions of him differed depending mostly on whether you lived in the North or in the South. He could kill anyone without a moment's hesitation, or he could show sympathy, kindness and even generosity to others—especially to people he sympathized with or who needed help. That was a strange mixture of character.

Though he was normally considered as an outlaw in hiding, he had many friends in high places, and it was some of those friends who he sometimes depended upon for favors and sometimes to help him evade the law.

The world that he was born into in 1847 was a place of great political unrest that was about to erupt into a long and violent civil war. It would tear this country apart and set the North against the South, brother against brother, father against son, and neighbor against neighbor! It was to be a dark and violent period in our history.

For many years, there had been a big and growing issue of both personal and national interests that hadn't been settled by politics or negations, but was destined to start a bitter Civil War in 1861. It would last for four long years. The issue was slavery, though it has traditionally been referred to as "States Rights."

Personal feelings and sentiments had grown deep and it divided this country into two parts, the North and the South. Only the Western Territories remained somewhat neutral; however some battles were fought as far west as New Mexico, and some violence even broke out in California.

The end of the war only ended the political issues, not the personal ones. Some of the resentments were evident for many years afterwards, especially in the South and also during the settlement of the American West. The South still resented the North and felt separate from it. Many of them still wanted to break away and form their own country again. Remember the old saying: "The South shall rise again!" Well, they really meant it. It was their 'battle cry'.

The KGC

In fact, many Southerners didn't consider that the war was really over, but it was just a temporary cease-fire until they could start it over again; and many were seriously preparing for it, including various groups and members of some organizations, including the secretive and powerful Knights of The Golden Circle (KGC).

Not much has been mentioned about the KGC after the turn of the century when they had failed to restart the Civil War. By then, most of their members had died out, but they had been a very large and powerful Confederate Organization that had a big influence on our history back then. They supported the Confederate Army and were accused of spying against the North and of committing acts of sabotage against it. Also, they were thought to be involved in the assassination plot that killed President Lincoln.

It would take a lot of money to finance another war, so the KGC accumulated and hid vast amounts of money, equipment and valuables around the country that they later abandoned when they were unable to get the war started again. It has been estimated to have been in the billions of dollars and the largest treasure ever hidden in our country. Treasure hunters have found a considerable amount of it and are still looking for more.

Born In Missouri in 1847

Jesse was born in Clay County, Missouri in 1847 near the little town of Kearney. His brother, Frank, was four years older, and they had a younger sister, named Susan. Their father had been a Baptist Minister and Jesse often sang in the choir and was even baptized. Their father had left in 1853 to join the California Gold Rush, but died of illness on the way. Their mother, Zerelda, married again a short time later, so Jesse and Frank had a stepfather, and later, a half-brother.

But when the half-brother, Archie, was only eight-years-old, he was killed during an attack on their home by a group of Pinkerton Agents who threw what has been variously described as a lighted flare or a bomb through the front window of their mother's house one night in an effort to flush out Jesse and Frank.

It exploded, either accidentally or on purpose, killed the young boy, seriously injured their stepfather, blew off the lower part of their mother's left arm, and started a fire. A gun battle then ensued in which Jesse and Frank escaped, and at least one or two of the Pinkerton Agents died from gunshot wounds the next day. Jesse and Frank gained a lot of public sympathy and support over the attack, and it brought a lot of criticism to the Pinkertons.

Incidentally, it may be noted that in most publications, it was reported that it was part of his mother's right arm that was blown off, while some others reported that it was her left. The photos of her showing the damage to her arm are tintypes, which shows things in reverse. It appears that it was her right arm, but actually, it was her left arm that was blown off; and that's how the mix-up started.

Also, some writers have stated that the tip of the middle finger on Jesses' right hand was missing. That missing fingertip was often mentioned as a distinguishing feature of Jesse—but actually, it was on his left hand. It appears that over the years some of the stories on Jesse James got a little further from some of the facts; so for the purpose of this book, information from the older and original publications, newspaper articles, and records, have been referred to.

Not much has been mention about their younger sister, except when she got engaged; Jesse was greatly opposed to it and threatened to commit suicide if she did. However, she did get married and Jesse didn't do as he had threatened.

Civil War Soldier

Jesse and his older brother, Frank, had fought on the side of the South during the war and were involved in some of the bloodiest and worst fighting in the war. They had been members of Quantrill's Raiders, a notoriously savage group that was often criticized for their ruthless attacks and raids on Kansas towns. Jesse was known for his acts of daring and bravery, and also as one of the best riders in the group. He was only 16 when he joined up.

Few wars have been fought with the passion and animosity as in our Civil War. And after it was over, that didn't stop all of the violence. The North wasn't through beating up on the South, and the South bitterly resented being ruled by the North. There were still old scores and personal grudges to settle, and Jesse and Frank were often victims of it, especially since they had been members of Quantrill's Raiders

Turned Bandit

Though he and Frank had tried to live peaceably afterwards, they found it was too difficult and thought society had turned against them; so they decided on another way of life—a life of crime, and once that started, there was no going back. They started a gang with Jesse as the leader. Bankers and shipping companies were all terrified of them since they had never been able to stop them. Any resistance would have been met with violence, which often happened. Jesse and his gang were always impatient and in a hurry.

One noted biographer wrote that Jesse and his gang pulled off about 26 daring robberies in and around Missouri for a total take of about half a million dollars. It's also been reported that Jesse and his gang stole more money than John Dillinger, Baby Face Nelson, and Bonnie and Clyde put together!

Man of Many Traits

Many things can be said about Jesse in addition to his intelligence and bravery. He was mischievous as a kid and was often described as a "Peck's Bad Boy." Sometimes, he was a flashy dresser and sometimes he wasn't. He had a sense of humor--but he also had a strong sense of justice and patriotism. After the war, he never forgot what happened to the South and to his friends; so most of his robberies were against railroads and banks that were owned or operated by northern interests.

He was clever, daring and completely fearless. He was quick on the draw and was an expert shot—considered by many as one of the best. He was always watchful and no man had ever been able to get the drop on him. That was an ability that he had been known for and an advantage that helped him survive many dangerous situations.

It is known that both Jesse and Frank were smart and well educated. They showed that in various ways. Frank was fond of Shakespeare, and would often quote from it. He also could understand and speak some German and Spanish. Jesse read several newspapers about every day to keep up with what was going on, and also to learn about any shipments of money or gold.

Frank was more conservative and not so impulsive; but he always stuck with Jesse. He often said that was because that he had to go along to protect his brother, and he did a good job of it.

Physically And Mentally Tough

Jesse was not only mentally tough, but also physically tough, and what he endured was remarkable. He had been shot on the right side of his chest during the Civil War. The bullet had punctured his lungs and it almost killed him. It had probably been from a .58 caliber musket ball. Whether the bullet had ever been removed or not, there seems to be no record. Also, Jesse had been shot in his leg once during one of his robberies.

The bullet wound to his lungs had remained open for a period of time that required daily treatments. Some thought that Jesse would die from it. However, his cousin, Zerelda Mims, who had the same first name as Jesse's mother, and who was related to her, nursed him back to health. During that time, Jesse fell in love with her and later they were married.

The hardships that Jesse often endured are hard to imagine. Sometimes riding hard throughout the day or night to escape from a posse; maybe through unfamiliar territory in wet or freezing weather and seeking shelter wherever he could find it without knowing for sure what to expect ahead--whether he would be welcomed, or shot at. He had to have been incredibly tough and determined— also extremely clever and very lucky. It took a man with his unusual ability and determination to do what he often did.

A Hunted Man

There was a big manhunt for Jesse and his gang that had gone on for years with a big reward offered for Jesse or Frank, dead or alive! But, nobody seemed to know where they were hiding, what they looked like, or what name they were using at the time. Jesse was a master of disguises and sometimes wore a short beard. He became very elusive and just melted into the environment.

One distinguishing feature between Jesse and Frank was height. Frank was about two inches taller than Jesse, and that was one way that helped identify them during robberies. So, sometimes Jesse would wear shoes or boots with high heels and wear a high hat to make him look taller, and Frank would wear low heels with a low hat, or cap, to make him appear shorter. That way they would both appear about the same height. But maybe, for the next robbery they would reverse the situation and Frank would appear much taller than Jesse.

Jesse was known for being clever and also imaginative. In addition to some of the disguises and tricks he used, there was another special one. An old blacksmith once said that whenever Jesse came riding to his shop, he always knew that Jesse wanted him to reverse the horseshoes on his horse in order to throw off and confuse anyone trying to track him after a holdup.

Reward Posters

One big problem of finding Jesse at the time was that very few photographs (tintypes) had ever been taken of him, and they could not be duplicated or reproduced on print like they can be today. So the reward posters out for Jesse didn't show a picture of him--only an artist's sketch printed from wooden blocks that were only a crude resemblance of him; therefore the public didn't really know exactly what he looked like in order to recognize him.

After each robbery, the gang would separate, spread out, and change their names. It was a good technique that worked for years. So, Jesse and Frank were always on the move and traveled around the country with a great deal of freedom. Very few people knew where they were or what they were doing until they pulled off another robbery someplace. The gang always wore masks during robberies and would give rebel yells as they rode off.

Jesse had many shoot-outs during his daring bank and train robberies, and also with some law enforcement officers like the Pinkerton agents, who for years had been desperately trying to capture or kill him. They concentrated on getting Jesse because he was the leader of the gang.

He was a big embarrassment to them and also to other law enforcement agencies that were trying to stop him, but always failed. That was largely due to the considerable amount of help and support that he and his brother received from his friends, the KGC, and other Southern sympathizers. They had good lines of communication and they always seemed to know where the law was and when they were coming to look for them.

There was a lot of intrigue involved in protecting him and his gang from the law. One historian described it as more like an intelligence system or a spy network. Actually, it was, and it was the KGC and it was far more extensive and insidious than thought. It was also connected to other secret and subversive organizations.

Jesse was considered a natural leader of men and also as a good judge of men, and that is credited with the amount of success he and his gang had for many years. Under different times, Jesse could have been a respectable member of society and contributed his part to it, but circumstances changed all that.

His Gang

His gang was carefully chosen and was described as close-knit. It consisted mostly of some distant relatives and other people he had known for years: such as the four Younger brothers, Cole, Jim, Bob, and John. They were long-time members of the gang and it has been thought that they were distant cousins on his mother's side of the family. Cole was the oldest and also quite famous on his own.

He had participated in the War and had a rather bloody record. He was ruthless at times, but could show compassion at other times. He had a sense of humor, was intelligent, and also very capable.

While in Texas, one time, he had a hand-to-hand knife fight with Sam Starr over the affections of Belle Starr. He won and Sam was badly wounded. Though he never married her, Belle had his daughter. Cole was an exceptionally rugged individual. He had 17 bullets still in his body when he died in 1915 at the age of 72.

Some other members of the gang were Wood Hite, a favorite cousin of Jesses', and Chell Miller who was later killed during the famous Northfield raid. Also, there was Jim Reed, who at the time was Belle Starr's husband. However, he was murdered in Texas by one of his partners in order to him.

Another member of the gang had been Ed Miller. However, Ed didn't know when to keep his mouth shut, especially after a drink, or two. When Jesse heard about that, he became quite worried, so Jesse, along with another gang member, Dick Liddil, tracked him down in another state and Jesse personally shot him.

Jesse was known to sometimes kill members of his own gang if he thought he couldn't trust them, became suspicious of them for some reason, or if they had carried out some robberies on their own without his permission.

Gads Hill Train Robbery

One of the more famous robberies that the gang pulled off was the Gads Hill train robbery in Missouri, in 1874. It was one of the first times a train had ever been robbed. After that, the Pinkertons redoubled their efforts to put an end to the gang and spread out in an effort to locate them.

John Younger, the youngest of the four Younger brothers, was considered the coldest and fastest gunman of the brothers, but was killed later on that year when he and his brother, Jim, met two Pinkerton Agents along a wooded trail in Missouri. The Pinkertons were looking for Jesse, but happened upon John and Jim. After a short conversation, a gunfight broke out and John was shot in the neck, but he stayed in the saddle long enough to kill both Pinkertons. However, in another version of the story, he only killed one while Jim shot the other one. John was the only one of the four Youngers to get killed, although his three brothers were badly shot up during their bandit years later.

John Wesley Hardin

There were seven men who participated in the big Gads Hill Robbery, and it was believed that one of the masked robbers was the famous John Wesley Hardin who has been credited with killing over 40 men in gunfights--more than any other Western outlaw.

He was deadly accurate with a pistol and after he had been released from prison, he gave public demonstrations of his incredible shooting ability. Many people said it was the best they had ever seen. But whether he was actually a member of Jesse's gang at that time, or at other times, is not certain.

An interesting note on John Wesley Harding is that while he was in prison, he studied law and later was admitted to the bar. But clients were afraid of his quick temper and of his reputation, so business was slow. He eventually was killed while playing cards by someone who sneaked up behind him and shot him in the back of the head, obviously by someone who didn't have the nerve to face him.

Also, Harding once had an interesting encounter in Abilene, Kansas with the famous, Wild Bill Hickok, the sheriff, who was noted as one of the fastest of all gunmen who had many notches in his gun handle. Hickok knew who Hardin was and after a few words were exchanged, he asked Harding for his guns. It's been said that Harding got the drop on Hickok by using the "reverse twirl." That was a trick that after presenting his guns with the handles forward, they were quickly twirled into firing position. Hickok then wisely decided to try diplomacy, and let Harding keep his guns if Harding promised not to use them while in town. He also invited Hardin to the local bar where they had a few drinks. Harding stayed around a little longer until he killed someone in a brawl at a local bar, and hurriedly left town that night.

Very Secretive

Jesse had been very secretive and told his secrets to no one. He once told a gang member that it was not a good idea to let too many people know what he was doing. He said that even his wife didn't know any of his business, and he didn't want her to know.

Also, since Jesse and Frank often bought and sold racehorses and had often bet on them at the racetrack, she might have thought that was his main business. However, she must have been suspicious at times! He also told some people that he was in the wheat speculation business.

Very few people, even some of those associated with him, knew who he was. It's quite possible that some of the men who rode with him sometimes didn't know who he really was since there were also a few other gangs who were active in the same area and they all wore masks.

Well Armed

At first, Jesse carried only one gun, but later, he carried two, plus a small hidden Derringer and also a rifle or a shotgun as well.

He once told Bob Ford: "If three men move in front of me, I will take all three before I fall!"

That being the case, many have wondered how it was possible that Bob was later able to get the drop on him and shoot him like he claimed he did?

Jesse was paranoid about someone getting the drop on him.

But when Jesse was at home, he was a loving husband and father, a church member and sometimes sang in the choir--but while using other names of course. Jesse had one son who became a noted attorney. He also had twin sons, but they died soon after birth. Jesse himself, carved out the tombstone for them.

America's Robin Hood

There are numerous cases on record where Jesse was very charitable. One is that he paid off a neighbor's overdue doctor bill with the proceeds of a robbery. Then stories began to circulate that some of the money he robbed was given to the poor and to some friends who were in need.

On time, he and Frank were credited with trying to help establish a school for black children. It happened one day when a noted black educator in Missouri was sitting on his front porch with a friend discussing ways to try to get a black school started when two men rode up and tossed a bag of gold coins up on his porch, and one said "Use that gold to start your school." They were pretty sure that it was Jesse and Frank James.

Another story that was widely circulated is that Jesse and a companion once helped the widow of an old friend who had just died. She now lived alone and penniless on a small farm. When Jesse and his companion, maybe it was Frank, were having lunch with her one day, they found that she was very upset and despondent because she was expecting the sheriff and a loan shark banker to come by that afternoon to foreclose the mortgage on her farm; and she didn't have the $500 that was owed, so she would lose the farm.

Before they left, Jesse gave her $500. and told her to be sure to get a full receipt for the money and a release of the mortgage. Later that day, Jesse and his companion held up the sheriff and the banker as they left. Jesse put the $500 back into his pocket and the widow got to keep her farm.

Due to frequent stories of such events, Jesse was often referred to as "America's Robin Hood" especially by many Southerners because it was said that he robbed from the rich and gave it to the poor, and that he took from the North and gave to the South. They also considered that he was still fighting the war for them, which in a way was true, and probably how Jesse and his gang thought to justify it.

Jesse's comparison to Robin Hood became very popular, and later even President Theodore Roosevelt said that: "Jesse was America's Robin Hood who took from the rich and gave it to the poor." Later, President Harry Truman, who was also from Missouri, was once quoted as saying the same thing when he said: "Jesse was America's Robin Hood who stole from the rich and gave it to the poor."

Being called a Robin Hood is another reason he has been memorialized in our history for over a century.

Members of The KGC

There are some good reasons to believe that Jesse, Frank, and some of the gang were important members of the KGC; but there is no way of knowing for sure because the KGC was a secret and unlawful organization, and there was never a listing of members, or suspected members, that was ever made public. Also, there doesn't seem to be any record that Jesse was a member, or claimed to be--or ever denied it.

Only a member knew who the others were around him. They had secret signs, secret passwords and secret handshakes, and there were severe penalties for letting secrets out.

So, in addition to what we already know about Jesse and the KGC, there are a few other clues to indicate that Jesse and Frank were members of the KGC, such as the references to "Castle James" that is mentioned in some of the accounts of the attack on the home of Jesse and Frank when the Pinkertons threw the bomb, or lighted flare, through the window that exploded. Meeting places for members of the KGC were referred to as "Castles."

Also, during some of their robberies, the gang wore Ku Klux Klan masks. The KKK was the military arm of the KGC. That could be further evidence that Jesse was a member of the KGC, and also that he stole on their behalf.

He and his gang stole hundreds of thousands of dollars, yet it was reported that he died almost broke since his wife had to sell some of his guns and other personal items to pay bills.

But there is an explanation to that. Most of the money and gold that he and the gang stole was buried as part of the KGC treasure to be recovered later to help finance another Civil War, so, the money really didn't belong to him, but to the KGC. Of course, he used part of it to live on.

A Jesse James Treasure Found

In fact, one of the treasures that Jesse and his gang had buried for the KGC was found in the Wichita Mountains, near Lawton, Oklahoma in 1936 by a treasure seeker by the name of Joe Hunter. He had used some old maps that had been made by Jesse himself to locate it.

Jesse had inscribed the names of all 11 members of the gang on an old brass kettle, declaring the treasure they had just buried there belonged to them all, equally. It was dated: "The 5th day of March 1876, The Year of Our Lord."

The names inscribed were: Jesse and Frank James, Cole Younger, Frank Miller, George Overton, Rub Busse, Charlie Jones, Uncle George Payne, Roy Baxter, Mack Smith, and Bud Dalton. Bud Dalton was also a member of the famous Dalton Brothers Gang!

The treasure was supposed to have been recovered later by the KGC, but somehow, that never happened. Joe Hunter always believed that he only found part of the treasure, which had contained some gold bullion, jewels, coins and an old watch. And apparently that was true because when Frank James got out of prison, he moved to Oklahoma to find the treasure himself, but since much of the terrain had changed, he could not locate the spot. He finally gave up and moved on to Missouri.

\The story of this treasure find was first published in the "Lawton Constitution" Newspaper in 1943. Information on this treasure, plus photos of Joe Hunter and the maps he used to find it are in my previous book: "Jesse James and Lost Treasures of The Knights of The Golden Circle," as listed on my website.

Jesse's Secret Life

Now, the question could reasonably be asked, if not actually assumed, that Jesse had a secret mission with the KGC and the Confederates after his supposed death to continue working with them towards their goal of starting another Civil War. If not, then what was he doing all of those years after the hoax of his death. There has been much speculation on that from many sources. Some researchers think they have recognized him in some group photographs taken many years later.

Considering the active and extreme lifestyle he had lived, it's not likely that he would have just retired to a quiet corner someplace and isolated himself. He had certainly been a rebel at heart and in action, and he fit in perfectly with the activities of the KGC. It's hard to imagine that Jesse just sat around someplace quietly during his later years. He could have still participated in some more robberies without being discovered; or at least, planned and organized them for other members of the KGC to carry out. It's hard to believe that he wouldn't have somehow continued on for as long as he could. Jesse was one who would never give up.

The Appeal of Bandit Life

In addition to the financial rewards of robbery, there were still another rewards, or appeals to it--ones that some people like Jesse could not resist.

Perhaps the famous bandit leader, Henry Starr, explained it best when he evoked the appeal of bandit life when he said: "Life in the open, the rides at night, the spice of danger, the mastery over men, the pride of being able to hold a mob at bay—it tingles in my veins. I love it. It is wild adventure!"

Another time, after he had been captured and was being held in jail in Chandler, Oklahoma, he said: "I must have excitement. I crave it. It preys upon me until I just step out and get into devilment of some sort." After his release, he continued robbing banks and was later shot to death while robbing a bank in Harrison. Arkansas.

Today, we would consider him as a "thrill" or "adrenaline junkie." Did Jesse also have that same attraction to it? It was like an addiction for some. The power of the gun was exciting and would have been hard to give it up from those who had experienced it. You have to admit that Jesse certainly lived that style of life and he did it frequently.

Volumes of books have been written about the exploits of many soldiers, politicians and others during the period of the Civil War, but the saga of Jesse James stands out mainly for what he did following the war—standing up and fighting back for what he believed in, and unwilling to give in to the North.

KGC In History

The story of the KGC is old news now, but they played an important and sinister role in our history during the 1800's. For those interested, there are a couple of books that were written during the 1860's that have been reprinted recently. They are:

"Knights of the Golden Circle, Treason History, Sons of Liberty, 1861," published in 1864 and again in 1903. It was written by Felix G. Stidger, a

Government Agent, who infiltrated their ranks and succeeded in bringing federal charges against some of their leaders who were sent to prison.

Another book, published in 1865, is entitled: "The Great Treason Plot In The North During The War." It gives information about the KGC and their part in the assassination of President Lincoln. A review of the book quotes: "Most dangerous, perfidious, extensive and startling plot ever devised; imminent hidden perils of the republic; astounding developments never before published."

Research can also bring up other articles and books. Including "The Secret And Mysterious Order of the Knights Of The Golden Circle," a book that I published in 2005 and available on the website: knightsofthegoldencircle.net

$500 REWARD

For the Arrest and Conviction of

JESSE JAMES

$25,000 REWARD
JESSE JAMES
DEAD OR ALIVE

$15,000 REWARD FOR FRANK JAMES

$5000 Reward for any Known Member of the James Band

Jesse James was the most wanted man in America for a number of years and there were remarkably huge rewards out for him--dead or alive. Also, there were rewards out for his brother or any other known member of his gang.

This is Jesses' mother, Zerelda Samuels, showing that part of her left arm was blown off (not her right arm as erroneously stated before.) It appears here that her right arm was damaged, but since this is a tintype photo, it shows things in reverse, including the buttons on her dress. Buttons on a woman's dress are always on the left side, while men's are always on the right side. The incident happened during a Pinkerton raid one night when a flare, or a bomb, was tossed through her window, and it exploded. They were looking for Jesse and Frank, but they were not there at the time.

The spirit of the woman is in the last two lines. "My boys were brave. I saw enough of it," she would say, laughing sharply. "I remember one day during the war Jesse and three more of Quantrell's men rode up to the house to wash. They told me Federals were chasing them, and my negro boy held the horses in the back while I watched from the front. By and by I saw about forty Federal soldiers going up through the field over toward old Dan Askew's house. Dan was a Northern spy. I shouted to Jesse:

"'I see some Federals.'

"'How many, mother?' asked Jesse.

"'About forty.'

"'Well, keep your eye on them, mother,' said Jesse, and they went right on washing.

"In a minute I saw them coming down toward our house and I shouted:

"'Boys, they're coming to the house.'

"Jesse was spluttering with his face down in the water basin, and he stopped long enough to say:

"'Let 'em come, mother; there are four of us, and I guess we can whip forty Federals all right enough.'

"I got scared and I ran back to where the boys were washing and I begged them to run.

"Jesse just laughed at me and said: 'Don't get rattled, mother. I'm not going away from here with a dirty neck if I have to fight two hundred and forty Federals instead of forty.'

"Well, sir, those four boys did not mount their horses till the soldiers were at the front gate and they heard the latch rattling. Then they sprang into their saddles and leaped the back fence and rode across the pasture like mad. The Federals galoped around the house, part one way and part the other, and pulled their cavalry pistols, and such shooting and cursing you never heard.

"Our boys shot back as they ran, and the last I saw of them was a waving line of horses going over the top of the hill. I waited half an hour and then I could stand it no longer. I got on my horse, Betsy, and went up over the hill, expecting to find the bodies of four boys shot full of holes. About a mile from the house someone hailed me from the brush.

"'Where are you going, ma?'

"It was Jesse, and he and the boys were coming down from the old schoolhouse, leading their horses and looking for their caps, which they had lost.

An interesting story about Jesse as told by his mother.

Chapter Two

THE BIG NORTHFIELD BANK ROBBERY AND SHOOTOUT

On September 7, 1876, there was a lot of excitement during a failed attempt by the James-Younger gang to rob two banks at once in the town of Northfield, Minnesota. Eight of the gang rode into town, two were killed there and another one killed later by a posse. Also, two of the town's citizens were killed and others wounded.

The eight-member gang had consisted of: Jesse and Frank James, the three Younger Brothers (Cole, Bob, and Jim), Bill Chadwell, Charlie Pitts, and Clell Miller. The gang had been visiting in St. Paul when they decided to rob two banks simultaneously in Northfield on their way home. That was a very ambitious plan and had never been attempted before, or since.

Jesse and Frank were veterans of many robberies, gun battles, and shootouts, but the one at Northfield was the one they were particularly noted for, and one that also came close to being their last.

The day before the attempted robbery, the gang rode into Northfield to check out the town and its two banks. That night, they stayed at a small tavern just outside of town and made their plans for the next day, which was to divide into two groups—one group for the first bank and the other for the second bank.

The first group consisted of five men: Frank James, Charlie Pitts, Bob Younger, Cole Younger, and Clell Miller. They would go to the First National Bank and rob it, while the second group would wait just across the bridge to watch and stand guard. If all went well, then the second group would go to the other bank and rob it. But, if the first group ran into trouble, then the other group would come to their rescue, and that is the way it turned out.

The first group went to the bank, tied up their horses in front, and three of them went into the bank, while the other two stood guard outside.

It should be noted that not all biographers agree on whether it was Frank or Jesse that went into the bank with the first group. Some claim that it was Jesse. However, according to statements by Cole Younger and several others later, they said that it was Frank and that it was Frank who had killed the bank teller. Cole also added that some of the gang had been drinking, including Frank, and that is mainly why things didn't work out as planned.

Things Go Wrong

Problems happened rather quickly at the bank when a bank teller told the bandits that the safe had a time lock on it. But in fact, it wasn't even locked and all the bandits had to do was to pull the handle and it would have opened.

An argument started when the clerks refused to open the safe. They were accused of lying and two of them were shot, one in the head by Frank James and the man died instantly. The only money they succeeded in taking was a sack full of money from an open cash drawer by Bob Cole.

Big Gun Battle

By that time, the citizens were alerted. Some of them had taken up arms and started shooting at the men as they were making their way out of the bank going to get to their horses. The horse belonging to Charlie Pitts was shot, so he was without his horse to make an escape. Later, he rode out double with one of the other gang members.

The three men who had gone into the bank had been caught in the open as they tried to return to their horses, so they took cover wherever they could and fired back at the people who were firing at them.

That alerted the members of the second group that consisted of Jesse James, Jim Younger and Bill Chadwell who had been watching from the far end of the street.

Lead by Jesse, they immediately went into action. They rode up and down the street, shooting left and right, yelling at the people to clear away from the street, and took shots at anyone who showed themselves.

It was one of the biggest and wildest shootouts in Western history.

At one point, there was a brief lull in the fighting as each side waited for the other side to make the next move. The gunfight was estimated to have lasted 20 minutes, or more, and that in its self is quite amazing.

By the time it was over, two members of the gang: Clell Miller and Bill Chadwell had been killed. The three Younger Brothers and Frank James had been wounded. One of the bank tellers was dead and the other was wounded. At least one person on the street was killed and some others were wounded. Only Jesse and Charlie Pitts escaped without being shot.

Their Desperate Ride To Escape

After the wild gun battle, the remaining bandits made a desperate escape from the town, which has been portrayed in several movies and documentaries that were pretty close to actuality, except there is no record of anyone riding a horse through a storefront window. But it was a thrilling stunt to watch.

What followed for the next two-and-a-half weeks was one of the most amazing and incredible events of human endurance, persistence, determination, will power, and pure guts that can ever be imagined!

It was the mad dash for freedom by the six remaining bandits: Jesse and Frank, all three of the Younger brothers, and Charlie Pitts. They were desperate and were driven far beyond what most men could possible endure. And it lasted for about two and a half weeks.

Chased By Posses

The story of the gang's dramatic race for freedom is a remarkable one itself—a story of grit, determination, suffering, and shootouts. As the gang rode out of town, they had left two of their companions dead behind them, Bill Chadwell and Clell Miller, and also one of their horses.

They knew that they might be shot, killed, or captured, or maybe die from exposure, or bleed to death. They were desperate men to begin with, but this made them even more so.

The gang rode at top speed, heading south towards home. They were severely handicapped because Bill Chadwell, who knew the trails and back roads out of town had been one of those killed. So, the gang had no one to guide them through the unfamiliar and wooded territory. That caused confusion and slowed them down a lot.

Also, Cole and Jim Younger were riding double since one of their horses had been killed during the gunfight. Two days later, they bought a horse from a farmer.

If they were captured, they knew they would be sent to prison for life, or maybe hanged! That was quite an inspiration to stop at nothing—to keep going, and kill anybody who tried to stop them! It was a matter of life-or-death for them!

These were no ordinary men, but hardened, Civil War veterans, accomplished bandits and bank robbers. They were smart, intelligent and expert quick-on-the-draw marksmen, and each one had killed more men than they could remember, and sometimes without hesitation or pity. They were undoubtedly the most dangerous and desperate men in America, and they were determined to escape!

To add to their problems, the weather had turned cold and drizzly and the gang was short on food. They were cold, tired, hungry, and also suffering from severe untreated bullet wounds that were leaving a trail of blood behind them. But that didn't stop them and they rode on. They knew that the telegraph wires were buzzing with information on where they had last been seen and what direction they had been going.

They got very little rest or sleep. Sometimes they slept in the saddle, but they could not stop or be caught asleep or off-guard. It was here that they put their military training and discipline to good use.

There is no evidence that they took shelter anywhere along the way, except once in a deserted farm house.

Bad conditions and bad luck were against them from the start. Also, the gang had been shot up rather badly.

The Wounded

Frank James had been shot in the thigh when he had run out of the bank building.

Bob Younger had been hit several times and was in bad shape. His right arm was useless since the bone in his right elbow had been shattered; also a bullet had lodged in his right thigh.

Cole Younger was bleeding badly from a number of bullet wounds. One bullet had broken his right elbow, another had lodged in his hip, and another in his shoulder. Later, he received some more bullet wounds during the final gunfight from the posse that finally captured them. In all, he had been shot 11 times-- making it some kind of a record.

It's incredible that anyone could survive after being shot that many times, but he did. In fact, he lived for many more years, and when he died in 1916 at the age of 72, he had a total of 17 bullets still in his body!

Also, it was reported that after Cole and his brothers were finally captured, Cole, though badly wounded by the 11 bullet wounds, would sometimes stand and bow to the ladies as he was taken back to town in a wagon. He was an extremely tough person, but also had a sense of humor.

Jim Younger Seriously Injured

But the one in the worst condition was Jim Younger and his story is really a sad one. He had been shot several times. One bullet had shattered his jaw and the bullet was still lodged in the upper part of his mouth. Blood gushed from the wound and he was suffering unbearable pain from it. It caused an impediment of speech, a disfigured face, and also forced him to eat only soft food. His life was full of pain and suffering after that. A few years later, while he and his brothers were serving a long term in prison, a fellow prisoner removed the bullet with a knife. Jim committed suicide14 years later.

Incidently, Jim had been shot in the arm a few years before in a gunfight when he and his brother, John, happened to meet with two Pinkerton detectives and a local sheriff while riding along a wooded trail back in Missouri in 1874. John was considered the fastest and best gunman of the four brothers, and though he was fatally shot in the neck, he stayed in the saddle long enough to kill the sheriff and one of the Pinkerton detectives.

Keeping Ahead Of The Posses

The gang often rode five, or six abreast, military style, like they had done during the Civil War. That way, they could all pull their guns together and shoot at once, if necessary. That gave them quick and deadly firepower and they blasted their way through numerous local posses sent out to stop them.

It must have been terrifying to anyone they met along the road to see this desperate band of six men who were dirty, blooded and ragged—riding or galloping five abreast in a military style formation.

Their guns were at the ready. They had no looks of friendliness--only of pain and determination on their faces. One quick look at them was enough for anyone to stand aside and let them pass and it was disastrous to anyone who tried to stop them.

Most history books have skipped over a lot of the details at this point, only referring to a few newspaper accounts. But the gang had numerous encounters with some local posses that attempted to stop or capture them. Usually there was an exchange of gunfire, but the attempts failed and the men rode on. They were more than a match for any posse twice their size!

Sometimes, they hid out in the daytime and traveled at night, or sometimes the other way around—whichever seemed best at the time. They never stopped to look for a doctor, although they all, except for Charlie Pitts and Jesse James, had received serious gunshot wounds and were loosing blood. Each day was a gamble as to how much further they could go because pursuing posses were never far behind, so they were forced to continue.

Shortly after leaving Northfield, they were seen galloping down the main street of the little village of Dundas, about three miles away, then they disappeared into the woods.

At Millersburg, they stole a horse for Bob Younger.

Four days later, they were spotted only 15 miles away from Northfield.

A few days later, they exchanged shots with a posse near Waterville.

At Shieldville, they surprised a posse who had just left their rifles leaning up against a barn. They held the men at bay while they watered their horses, then rode off and disappeared.

After two weeks on the run, they had succeeded in making their way to Mankato, about 60 miles from Northfield, where one of them went into town and bought some supplies.

After passing through Mankato, the gang was in bad shape and completely exhausted. You can easily imagine their dispositions. They were short tempered, were all in pain and disagreeable. Many angry words must have passed between them. Jesse was still their leader and had skillfully led their escape from the posses so far, but things were beginning to fall apart and there was quite a bit of dissention among them.

The Younger brothers had always stuck together under the leadership of Cole, but it was the good relationship between Cole and Frank James that had kept the gang together as long as it had. Cole's friendship with Frank had started back during the Civil War when they had fought together as members of Quantrill's Raiders.

Jesse Demands Bob Younger Be Left Behind

Finally, a few days after they had passed Mankato, Jesse had grown impatient at their slow progress. He blamed it on Bob Younger's condition for slowing them down too much and hindering their chances of getting away. At that point, he demanded that Bob be left behind—or shot!

That angered Cole and it started a serious argument that almost led to a gunfight between him and Jesse. It was only the pleas from the others that talked them out of it. It still might have happened if it hadn't been for the long friendship between Cole Younger and Frank James.

A Possible Gunfight Between Jesse and Cole Younger

What would have been the most famous and historic gunfight in Western history almost happened then. We can only imagine what the outcome would have been. Perhaps it would have ended the remarkable career of one, or both of them, as well as some of the others!

It was then decided that they would separate. Jesse and Frank would go their way and leave the three Younger brothers and Charlie Pitts to go on alone.

Jesses actions had made his brother, Frank, very angry. It was reported that he slapped Jesse in the face and said to him: "Don't ever make a remark like that again unless you want me to forget that I'm your brother."

However, Jesse was accurate in his assessment of the situation because a large posse was closing in on them. He and Frank departed that night—breaking through a line of pickets, riding double on a horse. If they had stayed with the others any longer, they would have been shot or captured.

Frank And Jesse Escape

But as they left, a shot was fired at them. The bullet passed through Frank's knee and lodged in Jesse's thigh. They then headed west towards Dakota Territory and disappeared. About two months later, they were back home in Missouri where Jesse had his wound treated by his old friend, Dr. Martin Yates.

That night, Jesse and Dr. Yates went out to dinner at a fancy hotel. They sat at a large table, where by coincidence, there just happened to be several Pinkerton agents who were on the hunt for Jesse. They didn't recognize him, but Jesse knew who they were and even delighted himself by having a short, casual conversation with them. It was a typical example of his bravado that he delighted in, but you can bet that Jesse had a gun handy.

End Of The Chase

Two days after Jesse and Frank had left the gang, the Cole brothers and Charlie Pitts had managed to make it to Hanska Slough along the Watonwan River, a location near Mandelia, about 25 miles east of Mankato. While hiding in a plum thicket and a short distance away from their horse, they were surrounded about daylight by a very large posse, headed by Sheriff James Glispin, who ironically, later became a good friend of the Youngers.

Unable to reach their horses, they tried to shoot their way out of the trap, but they were vastly out-numbered. A bloody gunfight began. Charlie Pitts, the only one who had been lucky enough not to have been shot before, was killed. All of the Youngers were hit again. One bullet struck Jim near his spine, and Cole was unconscious. Only Bob was still on his feet. Revolvers were no match against rifles.

Finally, Bob waved a white flag and said, "The boys are all shot to pieces. For God's sake, don't kill me!"

The men were then taken to the nearby jail at Faribault, where they were fed and their wounds treated. Later, they appeared before a judge, where rather than risk hanging, they all pleaded guilty. They were relieved when they received only a life sentence.

In all, the gang had successfully zig-zagged for about 150 miles across southern Minnesota in a little over two weeks while suffering many handicaps and while being pursued by over 100 people. They had never gone in the same direction for more that a couple of days.

Nothing like what they accomplished had ever been done before, and never has been since.

In later years, a question sometimes came up as to whether Jesse or Frank had really participated in the Northfield bank raid since they were not captured and never recognized by anyone in the posses. However, it's evident that they were there.

Cole Younger would never admit directly that the James boys had ever been with them on the robbery, and said that he blamed the failure of the robbery on several of his men being a little drunk and got too careless.

Model Prisoners

The Youngers were sent to the state penitentiary at Stillwater, Minnesota. They turned out to be model prisoners. In fact, they became well liked by the prison officials and respected by the other prisoners.

Cole was congenial and had a likable personality. He was intelligent, witty, a great conversationalist, and also a great practical joker. He had an interesting and varied past. He had not always robbed banks for a living. In addition to his wartime experiences with Quantrill's Raiders, he had worked in a variety of jobs, including as a government census taker in Texas. That is where he met Belle Starr. He also had been a member of a church there and had sung in the choir.

Bob was regarded as quite handsome—a lady's man as well as a man's man. He was 6 feet 2 inches tall and was regarded as an excellent specimen of manhood. In gunfights, he was considered brave and courageous. He had blue eyes, was well educated, intelligent, and had polite manners. His good looks had attracted the attention of many women. Though he never married, it was said that he could have had the pick of some of the most beautiful women around. Even while in jail, he was the recipient of many gifts of flowers, fruit, and baked goods from some ladies who came to visit him.

The Youngers gained somewhat of a celebrity status during their stay in prison. They received many visitors, often from reporters and historians. Many articles were written about them, mainly because they represented living examples of the last days of the wild west, bank robberies, gunfights, and the Civil War.

Released From Prison

Mostly due to publicity about the Youngers, efforts were started to gain their release. Even the warden and other prison officials helped promote it, and finally after 25 years, in July 1901, Cole and Jim were released. But it was too late for Bob. He had already died from his wounds.

Then, about a year later, Jim, who was still suffering from his wounds, had become despondent and committed suicide.

Cole had reformed and became somewhat of a celebrity. He traveled around the country for years and made a good living by giving talks on "What Life Has Taught Me." My father once saw him on the street at Alva, Oklahoma in about 1914, where my father and his parents lived before I was born there. Cole finally died in March of 1916.

On an interesting side note—Cole's long barreled, nickel-plated, ivory-gripped .45 Colt Revolver that was taken from him when he was captured, was sent to his old girl friend, the notorious female Bandit Queen, Belle Starr, at his request. He had once lived with her for several years while in Texas and had fathered her daughter.

For several years after the Northfield Raid and while the Cole brothers were still in prison, things had been pretty quiet and nothing much had been heard about Jesse or Frank James—although some small robberies had occurred that were blamed on them, but it was hard to tell since the robbers always wore masks.

Actually, Jesse and Frank had moved to Nashville, Tennessee for a while since they figured everybody would be looking for them in Missouri.

It wasn't until late 1879, three years after the big Northfield raid, that Jesse and his wife decided to move back to Missouri. And it was not long after that with Jesse back in familiar territory that he began planning on resuming his old line of business, so he started to form up a new gang.

This is the First National Bank Building in Northfield, Minnesota that the James-Younger Gang attempted to rob in 1876, but was fought off in a big gun battle with the citizens. One bank teller was killed plus one citizen. Two of the gang members were killed and most of the others were wounded. After two weeks of fleeing from posses, one more gang member was killed, and the Cole brothers were captured and sent to prison. Jesse and Frank escaped, but were wounded doing so.

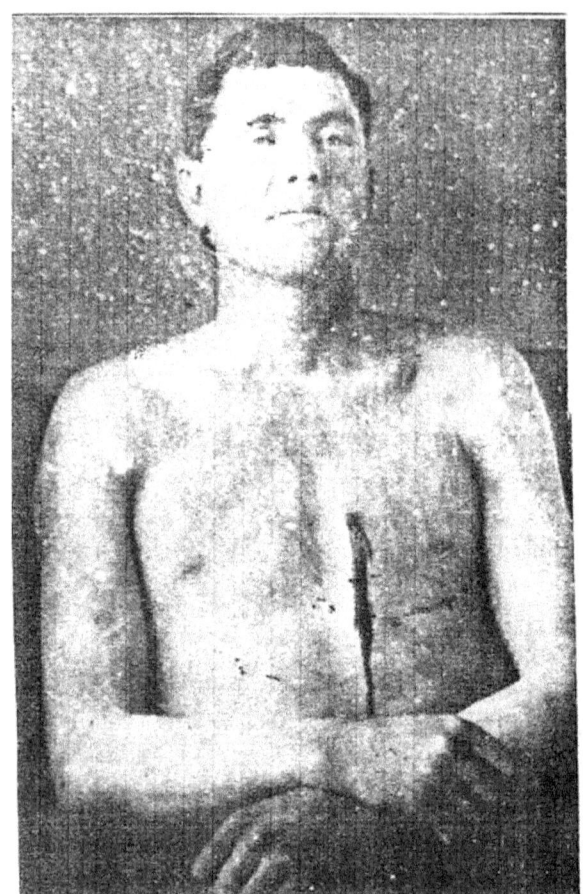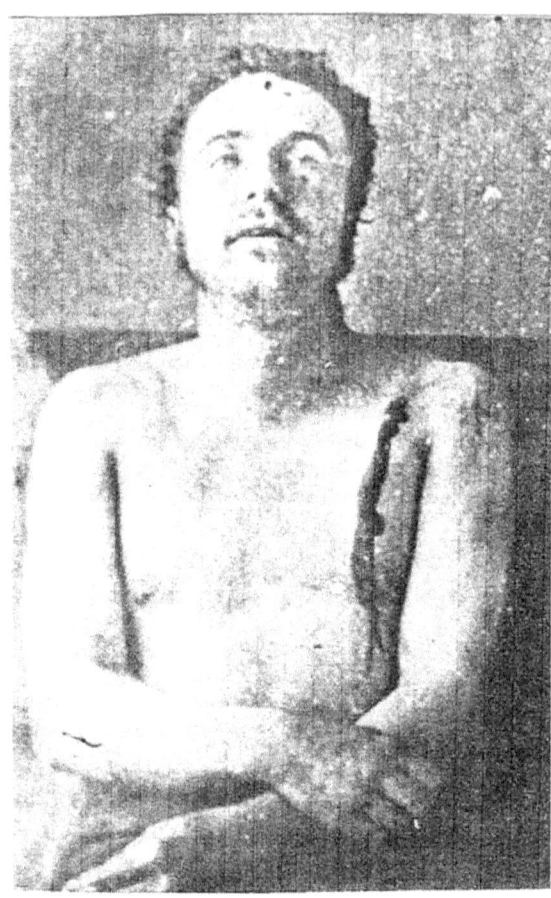

Above: Chell Miller and Bill Chadwell (alias William) killed during the shootout at Northfield; and Charles Pitts, below, killed by a posse about two weeks later.

Cole Younger

Jim Younger

Bob Younger

Pictures of the three Younger brothers in prison after they were captured following the big Northfield bank robbery and shoot-out.

 This is the last photo of Cole Younger shortly before his death in l916 at age 72. It shows what appears to be a very friendly and peaceful man. But looks are deceiving in this case because he had led a very violent life. (He had 17 bullets still in his body when he died.) He was known for his quick temper and for killing many innocent people during bank robberies. He was a main member of the James/Younger gang, along with his two brothers. He would have surely killed Bob Ford in revenge for assassinating Jesse James unless he knew the whole thing was a hoax to help Jesse escape from the law.

Chapter Three

BOB FORD CLAIMS HE KILLED JESSE JAMES

One of the biggest and most unusual hoaxes that ever happened in our country occurred in April 1882, in St Joseph, Missouri. That was when Bob Ford, one of Jesse's new gang members that nobody had ever heard of before, claimed he had just killed Jesse James by shooting him in the back of his head after Jesse had taken his guns off!

He said he had done it to collect the big reward money.

A National Sensation

The story came as a big surprise and it was soon a national sensation. It was the biggest and most controversial story since the end of the Civil War and the public could not read enough about it, especially since they had not heard much about Jesse after the big Northfield bank robbery and shootout several years before.

Jesse had been keeping quiet and nobody knew where he was hiding. The three Cole brothers were still in prison and Frank James was hiding out in Tennessee, so not much had been mentioned about Jesse or of his gang in recent years. Although some small robberies had occurred that were blamed on them, it was hard to tell since the robbers always wore masks.

Some thought that maybe Jesse had reformed, or had left the country, or maybe had died someplace—and that's probably what Jesse hoped they were thinking.

Was Hard To Believe

So, when the public heard about the shooting, they were shocked. They found it hard to believe that Jesse, the notorious and bigger-than-life outlaw, who for over 15 years had been able to come out of nowhere with his gang, pull off daring robberies of a train, bank or a stagecoach--often with shooting and killing, then successfully escape and hide from the law, could have been killed in his own home in such a strange and unexpected way. It just didn't make sense and some people didn't believe it. They thought it was all an elaborate hoax.

Large Reward

There had been a very large reward posted for Jesse, $20,000 dead-or-alive, and it was expected that some sheriff, Wells-Fargo or Pinkerton Agent would eventually track him down; or that he would be caught by a posse, or killed in a shoot-out. But to hear instead that he had been killed in such an unlikely and cowardly manner was hard to believe. It was not like Jesse to put himself in a situation without a chance to defend himself. There had to be more to the story—and there was!

Few Knew What Jesse Looked Like

Not many people knew what Jesse looked like except for his family, some gang members and a few friends. He was a master of disguises and always had lived under a false name. At the time of the shooting, he was going under the name of Thomas Howard. Before that, he had used the name of Johnston, and before that, had used various other names.

He also had moved around the country a lot. Just after the famous Northfield raid, he and Frank with their families had moved to Nashville, Tennessee since they figured everybody would be looking for them in Missouri. It wasn't until 1879 that Jesse and his wife decided to move back to Missouri. During that time, he had been able to keep himself out of the public eye. So, the public was greatly surprised when they heard the astonishing story.

A swarm of criticism immediately arose against Bob Ford after his story had been published in the newspapers. He was accused of being a "Judas" and many people had nothing but the utmost contempt for him, and also against the people who tried to make a hero and law-abiding citizen out of him.

There was even a popular opinion poll in which Bob was voted as "the most contemptible coward ever to go unhanged!"

Jesse's New Gang

When Jesse decided to start up a new gang, that is when he asked Bob and Charles Ford to join him. But it was without Frank because Frank was still hiding out somewhere in Tennessee.

Charles Ford, who was Bob's older brother, had already helped Jesse pull off a few robberies. It's not clear whether the three of them had ever worked together on any robberies, or not.

Bob had said that Jesse wanted to know them better before they did some work together, so Jesse invited the two of them to spend some time at his house. It was a big house on a little hilltop on the edge of town with seven rooms and a stable close behind it. It also had a strong, wooden, rail fence all around it.

Bob also said that Jesse had told him that he had rented the house because it was situated on a little hilltop so that if 100 men came after him, he could hold them off until he could get to the stable and ride away from any pursuers. One law official later described the house as certainly being able to withstand a siege.

That was an example of how Jesse's mind worked. He was always thinking ahead to give himself as much of an advantage as possible, and that's one reason he was able to pull off as many robberies as he did and still escaped from the law.

Bob's Strange Stories

Bob's explanations of how he had shot Jesse were very strange and hard to believe. They certainly appeared to have been hastily made up at the time and too absurd and improbable to be true—ones that he also had a hard time keeping straight when he told them later. Some of them were noticeably contradictory, and during the first day, he changed part of his story three or four times.

Undoubtedly, someone was killed, but there are many reasons to believe that it was not Jesse, but was someone else instead, and that it was part of a carefully planned scheme so that Jesse could escape from the law and the Ford brothers could claim the reward money.

That Morning

That morning, according to Bob, the three of them had been out in the stable behind the house for a while to curry the horses. Then they went into the house for breakfast.

After breakfast, he said that his older brother, Charles, had stayed in the kitchen to help Mrs. James with the dishes, while he and Jesse went into the front room to talk. Bob claimed that Jesse was very upset at him because he had not told Jesse of the recent arrest of Dick Liddil, one of Jesse's friends, and that an argument started between them.

Jesse Takes His Guns Off

Then, he claimed that Jesse unexpectedly broke off the argument and did a very strange thing. He walked over to the bed and deliberately unbuckled his two belts carrying his four revolvers and tossed them on the bed in front of them. Then Jesse removed a small pocket pistol and tossed it on the bed also.

Bob added that it was the first time that he had ever seen Jesse without his guns on. But what is even stranger, he said that Jesse removed "four" revolvers from his belts that were tossed on the bed. Now, who would carry four revolvers in his gun belts? That was unheard of. The bulk and the weight would have been too heavy and cumbersome for any gunfighter. Possible Bob was misquoted, or else it was part of his imaginary story that he made up.

It was known that Jesse really didn't trust anyone, so he always wore his revolvers—even inside his own home, and would never take them off. Sometimes, he would draw his revolvers and peek out of a window to watch someone if they got too close.

Stood On a Chair

Then Bob described how Jesse picked up a feather duster from the table and said that the picture above the door was awful dusty. So, he picked up a chair, placed it in the doorway, stood upon it with his back to Bob and started to dust the picture frame.

Bob later remarked that even he didn't see any dust on the picture. Jesse's wife had always been an immaculate housekeeper.

It has often been wondered why Jesse (as Bob told it) would have stood on a chair to dust off the picture frame when he could have easily reached it without the chair. That has been an eternal mystery because the ceilings of the house were low.

Bob Sees His Chance

Bob said it was then that he saw his chance to shoot Jesse when Jesse was standing on the chair with his back turned--unarmed. So, he quickly drew his revolver and fired. He also said that when Jesse heard the click of the hammer being pulled back, he quickly started to turn his head, but it was too late!

Bob claimed that his brother was still in the kitchen helping Mrs. James, and when they heard the shot, they both ran into the front room to see Jesse dead on the floor.

From that point on, it was pandemonium!

Bob and Charles quickly ran out of the house and into the street. They yelled out that they had just killed Jesse James.

That started a lot of excitement and confusion!

It also could have been a diversion away from the house, giving Jesse a chance to disappear while leaving a dead body in the front room.

We will never know for sure, but there is reason to believe that the victim was not killed in the front room, but was killed in the stable, then dragged into the house. And we will never know for sure who shot him, but evidence points to Jesse himself.

When Bob and Charles ran out into the street, they asked the people to notify the police. Then Bob went to the telegraph office and sent telegrams to Governor Crittenden, the local sheriff, and others. Then he and Charles went to the city jail to give themselves up.

What Have You Done

According to the newspaper reports of what was said just after the shooting, Mrs. James screamed at Bob to come back, and asked: "What have you done?"

He replied: "I swear to God I did not do it! Then he later told her it was an accident and the gun went off accidentally!

In another report of the incident, Mrs. James yelled at Bob and Charles as they ran out of the house: "What have you done?"

Bob yelled back: "No! We didn't kill him!"

It's very strange that Bob would have said that at first, then later say the opposite!

Those comments were well documented in the newspapers of what Bob had said immediately after the shooting--though he later changed his story to say that he had indeed killed Jesse James; then changed his story again to claim that his brother was also in the room when he shot Jesse.

Why was he telling different stories at different times?

If the first reports of what Bob said to Jesse's wife are accurate, it could indicate that the actions that morning happened rather suddenly and unexpectedly, and that Bob was making up the stories as he talked. Also, that the shooting happened before anyone had a chance to tell Jesse's wife what was going on, so naturally, she would have been taken by surprise.

Jesse was always very secretive and had said that he never discussed his plans or business with his wife. So, understandably, she would have been surprised and reacted that way, at first—until she was tipped off that it was a hoax and that she was supposed to act like the dead person was her husband.

Jesse's Wife Did Not Weep

Then, according to the newspaper reports, Jesse's wife went over, held Jesse's head in her lap and tried to wipe away the blood. As she did, she took the matter in a "cool and philosophical way and did not weep."

That appeared to be rather strange to those first on the scene, and they made it a point to remark about it.

It was known that she was a loving and affectionate wife. They had been married for seven years and had two children (she also was a first cousin). It would be expected that she would weep bitterly—but she did not!

Was that because she had just then realized that it was a hoax, and not Jesse, but someone else who had been killed? Otherwise, it would have been expected that she would have wept bitterly.

She had demonstrated her love and affection for him numerous times, including when she had spent weeks nursing him back to health before they were married when he was suffering and almost died as a result of a serious gunshot wound to his chest that he had received during the Civil War.

Maybe the wound explains why Jesse was often irritable and quick tempered.

Jesse Was Always Alert

Jesse had always been very careful and cautious about being taken by surprise. Some said that he was paranoid about it, and that he was always on guard from anybody who might be tempted by the huge reward, so he was very watchful and always armed, even in his own home; and at night he slept with two loaded guns by his side.

Fast On The Draw

Jesse was known for being very fast on the draw, and no man had ever beat him to it.

In fact, Charles Ford had remarked several times about it when he said: "Jesse was always watchful and no man could ever get the drop on him."

He also said that Jesse had once told him, "If three men move in front of me, I will take all three before I fall!"

With that being the case, then how did this young, inexperienced man, who was only 21 years of age and not a gunfighter, get the drop on Jesse so easily?

Bob's explanation made it sound like Jesse had been foolish, or stupid enough to have taken his guns off, then unexpectedly stood on a chair and turned his back towards him? That would have left Jesse completely defenseless.

But, Jesse had not lived as long as he had by being stupid or careless!

Jesse had never done anything like that before--putting himself in a position where someone could have taken advantage of him. That was just too unbelievable…especially to those who knew Jesse--or who had ever faced him!

It's been recorded that Jesse had killed at least 23 men and it was known that no man had ever been able to catch him off-guard. But Bob Ford claimed that he had, and that's one reason many people didn't believe his story.

Questions And Doubts

Skepticism was soon spreading about Bob's story. Many believed that it wasn't Jesse who had been killed; but was someone else, and that it was more likely part of a hoax so that Jesse could escape from the law.

Questions were also being asked about who was really killed, though the dead man was similar to Jesse and was about the same size and about of the same age, and both had a short beard.

Although the dead man was said to be Jesse by the Ford brothers, Jesse's wife, the local sheriff and some others, that still wasn't enough to convince everybody.

The Mysterious Dead Man

However, there was a dead man in Jesse's front room that was said to be Jesse. But not everybody believed it, so questions persisted about who the dead man was?

But, if it wasn't Jesse—then who was it? Nobody seemed to know for sure!

That soon became a big question, and it has been for years!

Some thought that Jesse was still alive and claimed they had reasons to think so. Some said that Jesse was trying to pull off another hoax like he had tried before, and that the Ford brothers and Jesse's family were playing their part in it.

While the body was in the coroner's office, it was claimed to be Jesse by his wife and a few others who said they knew him. Jesse's mother arrived the next morning at nine o'clock, and went directly to Jesse's house first and talked to Jesse's wife.

Then she went to the morgue and agreed that it was her son. As for Jesse's older brother, Frank, he was not there at the time—which was convenient and kept him out of the scene.

Who Was Bob Ford

There were also a lot of questions being asked about Bob Ford. Who was he? Had he killed anyone before? Was he a known criminal, or robbed any banks? What kind of a person was he? Had he been in any gunfights before? If not, and there seemed to be no substantial records on any of these, then how could such a person succeed in killing Jesse James after so many other people had tried before?

Body Was Similar

The body of the dead man happened to resemble Jesse enough that it could be mistaken for Jesse, provided you didn't know exactly what Jesse looked like. And very few people outside of his small gang and his family knew that.

In the meantime, a big debate was going on between those who thought Jesse was dead and those who thought he was still alive, and there were numerous stories in the newspapers about it.

Then, something most unusual happened!

Governor Declares Jesse Was Killed

While the body was still in the coroner's office, the Governor of the state, Thomas T. Crittenden, unexpectedly stepped in on the second day and made a public announcement—declaring that it was Jesse who had been killed and that the country was now rid of him and his gang! He also sent a telegram on that day to the coroner telling him that it was Jesse's body there in his office and should be identified as such.

That was like a commanding officer giving orders to a sergeant with the sergeant expected to act accordingly. In this case, it was the State's senior officer giving instructions down the line to the coroner, and maybe he also mentioned some of the reward money because the Governor later admitted in court that he had given a lot of money to others involved for their cooperation.

The Governor's actions surprised a lot of people and many wondered why he would get involved and make such a surprising announcement. After all, Jesse's family and friends had already said that the body was Jesse's!

For the Governor to get involved at this time seemed like an extraordinary action for a high-ranking, state official, like a Governor, to do--and actually, it was!

Also, how could he be so sure that it was Jesse--especially since he had not gone to St. Joseph to see for himself? That in itself was rather suspicious.

Why The Governor Acted

The Governor's announcement that it was Jesse was very unexpected, but he had some good reasons for doing that.

One involved a political issue--but perhaps the most important was to put a quick and official end to the incident before it could be discovered that Jesse was not the man in the morgue.

If that were to happen, it would prove that Jesse was still alive and that would had led to an investigation with serious and far-reaching results because it would then be necessary to find out who the dead man was, and who killed him, and why. That could expose a number of people in addition to the Ford brothers—including the Governor himself in the involvement of killing an innocent man!

That would lead to murder charges being filed for the murder of an innocent man--but if so, against who? It wasn't known yet that the Governor had some secret meetings with the Ford brothers.

Also, if the hoax had been discovered, Jesse would have been back on the run again and the Governor would be under attack again. So, it was a win-win situation for both. Also, the history of Jesse James would read quite differently today!

The Governors' Campaign Promise

When the Governor was running for office a few years before, there were some demands by some to put an end to the James Gang. The Governor thought that would be to his political advantage to say that he would; so like a typical politician, he promised that if elected, he would do that. After all, a Governor is supposed to stand for law and order.

Of course, he hoped that in the meantime the situation would somehow be resolved--that Jesse would probably be caught or killed and he wouldn't have to deal with it. But after he had been in office for over two years, it looked like that was not going to happen and the Governor was being criticized by some for not keeping his promise. That is one reason the Governor wanted to convince the public that he had kept his promise and that Jesse was really dead.

Jesse had been very elusive after the famous Northfield raid. Nobody knew where he was hiding. He had become a big embarrassment to law officials who had been trying to capture or kill him, especially the Pinkerton Agents.

Jesse And The Governor Were Old Friends

It was common knowledge though, that Jesse and the Governor had been old friends. Both had been strong Southerners and they had previously worked together on some business matters. Jesse had once hired him to be his attorney and had also contributed to his campaign funds. That suggested to some that the Governor was dragging his feet on his promise, and that was probably true.

So with the Governor under attack from some of his political opponents and being criticized by some of the newspapers and law enforcement departments for not keeping his promise, he needed to find a way to solve the situation—and he did, secretly, with the Ford brothers.

The Governor's Secret Deal With The Fords

It was not known until later when the Ford brothers went to trial that they had secretly met with the Governor several times with what was described later by the newspapers as a "secret plan to kill Jesse James," and that he had also agreed to give them the reward money and if they were found guilty of murder, he would pardon them—which he did.

When the news of his secret deal with the Fords was exposed during the trial, it became a big story; actually more like a scandal, that the Governor had condoned a plan to assassinate anyone—even a wanted man. Many people were shocked about it, and rightfully so.

Official records of this secret deal between him and the Ford brothers can still be found in most of the historical accounts of Jesse James, and in some of the old newspaper reports.

Obviously, the Governor wanted to make it 'official' that Jesse was dead and to get the body buried as soon as possible before the hoax and his part in it could be exposed. That there was a secret deal between him and the Ford brothers is the explanation as to why Bob Ford immediately sent a telegram to the Governor right after the shooting to say that they had killed Jesse.

Secret Meetings Never Denied

It's most interesting that the Governor never denied that the Ford brothers had secretly met with him several times, not only about how they planned to kill Jesse (or to make it look like they had) but that he had also agreed to give them the reward money and also to pardon if necessary. However, there were other people who also received some of the reward money but the Governor never said who they were.

The Ford brothers felt that they needed some protection and assurance that they wouldn't be prosecuted for murder, and also that they could collect the reward money.

It's most likely that Jesse was also in the middle of the plan, and had his own ideas as to how it would work out, as explained more in the next chapter.

An interesting point to consider here is that neither of the Ford brothers had the nerve to have a shoot-out with Jesse, and they never intended to, since they both knew how dangerous that would be, and all who had tried it before had been killed.

Body Was Guarded

While the issue was going on over whether Jesse had really been killed, or not, the body was kept in the coroner's office under guard. The public was not omitted. Only family members, some close friends and some officials were allowed to see the body. There it was kept until some officials and friends of Jesse arrived who took charge of the body and transported it to his mother's home for burial in the family plot in his mother's front yard. There had been no funeral.

Finally Buried

During the trip, the body was under close guard so that nobody viewed it. There were reports that the body might be stolen, kidnapped, or maybe destroyed by some people who hated Jesse. Though hundreds of people went to see the burial, there is no record of anything unusual happening.

With that, plus the Governor's declaration that it was Jesses who had been killed, the issue was, as they say, "Dead and buried!"...At least, it was for a while!

Since the Governor had made it official that it was Jesse, that's how it was reported in the newspapers and also later in the history books. After all, who could argue against what the Governor had declared!

Bob And Charles Ford Go On Trial For Murder

Since Bob Ford had readily admitted that he had shot Jesse James, along with some help from his brother, they both were charged with "Murder In The First Degree" by a Grand Jury, and during the first day of their trial, they were quickly found guilty and sentenced to be hanged!

Governor Intercedes And Pardons Them

But, strangely enough (or maybe not) just two hours after the sentence was announced, the Governor sent a telegram to the court to pardon them on all charges and to set them free--just as he had promised them that he would do!

The Governor's quick and strange actions have always been considered as collusion between him and the Ford brothers. That was rather shocking and unexpected by most of the public, and some were asking, why?

But, since the body had been buried rather quickly and without delay, the official investigations were over.

The Myth

However, that did not put an end to the controversy. The story of Jesse James has been told and retold over the years in books, movies and TV, until it has become a myth in our history. But the more the circumstances are investigated today, the more convincing it becomes that it was actually just that—a myth, and that Jesse had not been killed!

Should History Be Rewritten

In view of some of the new information that we now have, there are a number of researchers and some Western historians who now agree with the old and consistent rumors from people who claimed that it wasn't Jesse who was killed, but was instead, a hoax perpetrated on the American people.

They think that history should be rewritten—and perhaps it is.

Events Later

The lives of the Ford brothers afterwards were destined to be turbulent and full of controversy. Sometimes, they were praised, and sometimes they weren't. Some people thought they were heroes, while others thought they were cowardly villains.

For a year or more, Bob and Charles often made public appearances on stage—acting out how they had killed Jesse James. That was very popular for a while, and they received $100 per night. But it eventually became old news and often they were "booed" by some in the crowd, and in a few cases were threatened to be hanged!

It was generally thought by some that Frank James would suddenly appear and take revenge on the Fords, but that didn't happen. And there was at least one person who predicted that he wouldn't. He was James Timberlake, the sheriff of Clay County, and an old friend of Jesse and Frank.

Timberlake was also the one who had taken charge of the body to escort it back to his mother's home for burial—presumably as an Honor Guard, but actually to protect the body to make sure that nobody examined it to find out that it was not Jesse! Obviously, he was in on the hoax and knew that Frank would not come to kill Bob or Charles Ford.

Interestingly enough, that was very true. A few years later, after Frank had been pardoned of his crimes by Governor Crittenden, Frank was asked by a reporter why he didn't hunt down Bob Ford for murdering Jesse.

Frank replied that he could understand it and really didn't blame Bob for doing that because of the temptation of the large reward money. That was a good answer to give, considering he knew that Jesse had not been killed.

Bob Ford Murdered

Eventually, Bob moved on to Creed, Colorado. There, he bought and operated a saloon until he got into an argument with Edward O'Kelly who shot him to death with a shotgun in June, 1892.

Some reports were that it was an argument over a diamond ring, or jealously over a woman; but others think it was in retaliation for Bob having killed Jesse James.

Charles Ford Said to have Committed Suicide

Bob's older brother, Charles, also had problems. We are not sure exactly what they were, maybe depression since he and his brother did not become national heroes like they thought they would, but instead were often hated and criticized--also, being disappointed for receiving only a small amount of the reward money.

He was found shot to death in his room one day about four years later, but under some strange circumstances. Some speculated he had been killed to keep him quiet, while some thought he was killed by a Jesse James partisan.

Frank James Surrenders

Six months after Jesse was supposedly killed. Frank James surrendered to Governor Crittenden. The details that Frank James had worked out for his peaceful surrender have never been revealed, but there had been a lot of correspondence between them. The Governor told Frank that he couldn't promise amnesty, but did promise that if he would give up his outlaw activities and lead a peaceful life, he would make sure that he would get a fair and impartial trial.

So, on the afternoon of October 5, 1882, Frank, accompanied by one of the gang's old friends, John Edwards, walked into the Governor's office in the Capitol building to surrender.

Edwards then said to the Governor: "I want to introduce you to my friend, Frank James."

After the two exchanged greetings, Frank removed his pistol and cartridge belt, and said: "I want to hand over to you that which no living man, except myself, has ever been permitted to touch since 1861, and to say that I am your prisoner."

Since it had been prearranged, there were numerous state officials and newsmen present who immediately crowded around Frank to shake his hand and to interview him. It was an incredible scene for the rest of the afternoon as Frank related some stories and also solemnly told them that now, he knew that crime didn't pay and was glad that a new day was beginning. The Governor was reported as smiling and beaming through it all.

It was a very impressive occasion and was described in the newspapers as more like a "big social event." Some even made it appear more like the State had surrendered to Frank, instead of Frank surrendering to the State!

It was decided that Frank and his friend, Edwards, would stay that night at a fancy local hotel until the next day when Frank would be turned over to the sheriff of Jackson County.

Frank's Pardon

Rather unexpectedly, Frank was fully pardoned for all of his crimes by the Governor. That was eight months after the same Governor had pardoned the Ford brothers. Frank then bought a farm near Fletcher, Oklahoma, where he spent a lot of time looking for the rest of the treasure that he, Jesse, and the rest of the gang had buried there in 1876. But apparently, he never found it. He died of natural causes in 1915 at the age of 72.

On a curious note…Frank had remarked several times that he was afraid that after he died, his body would be dug up for scientific research on his brain. He was adamant about trying to make sure that didn't happen, so he directed that his body be cremated, which it was and the ashes buried in the family plot.

He also said he had the same fears about any post-mortem or scientific research being done on Jesse's remains. Obviously, he said that because he figured that if they did, they would discover that the body wasn't that of Jesse and the hoax would be discovered and Jesse would be on the "Wanted List" again.

Jesse's Son

Jesses' son, also named Jesse, became a lawyer, and was often in the news, especially in 1898 when he was accused of leading a gang on a train robbery. He was brought to trial, but was found not guilty.

Jesse's Mother

Jesse's mother, Zerelda, was always in the limelight. She was often interviewed and photographed. She opened her home to visitors much of the time, and often, she would sell pebbles from her son's grave for fifty cents. And if she ran out of them, she would find some more somewhere.

She sometimes would visit her son, Frank, on his farm in Oklahoma. She died February 10, 1911 in a Rock Island passenger train about 20 miles out from Oklahoma City on her way back to her home in Clay County, Missouri. She was 86-years-old and had been in bad health for a while. She was accompanied by her daughter-in-law, Ann Ralston James, who was Frank James's wife

Ann lived for many years afterwards and was sometimes in the news. She was especially known for her remark that "The true secret of Frank and Jesse James would die with her!" and she never revealed what it was!

There has much speculation about that and what she knew that the rest of us didn't.

Bob Ford, above left, claimed he had killed Jesse James with the help of his older brother, Charles, below.

 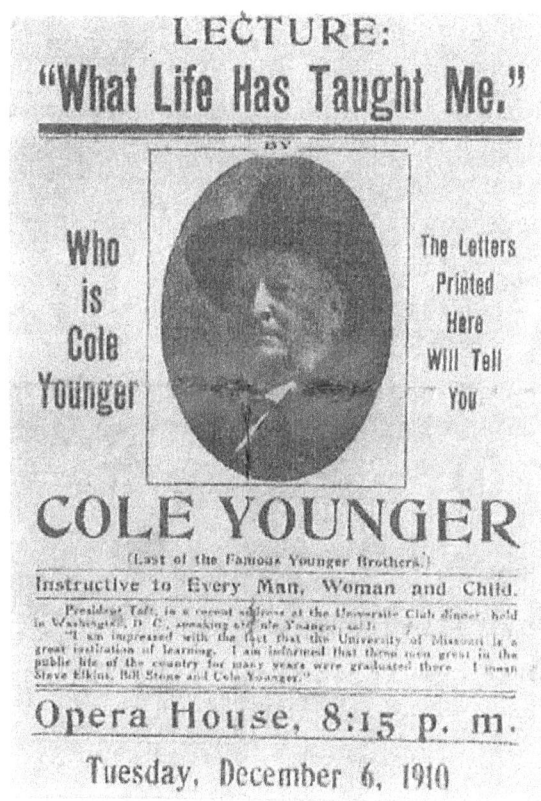

Left: One cartoonist pictured Jesse as an angel for the South. Right: After he was released from prison, Cole Younger was a popular speaker around the country.

This is the house in St. Joseph, Missouri where Jesse and his family were living when he was supposedly shot in the back of his head by Bob Ford on April 3, 1882. **It** was said to have happened in the room on the left. The house was very small.

This is the famous sketch that was widely published in 1882 showing how Bob Ford shot Jesse James. But according to the records, Bob had said that he was alone in the room with Jesse at the time and also was seated in a chair, not standing up, when he fired.

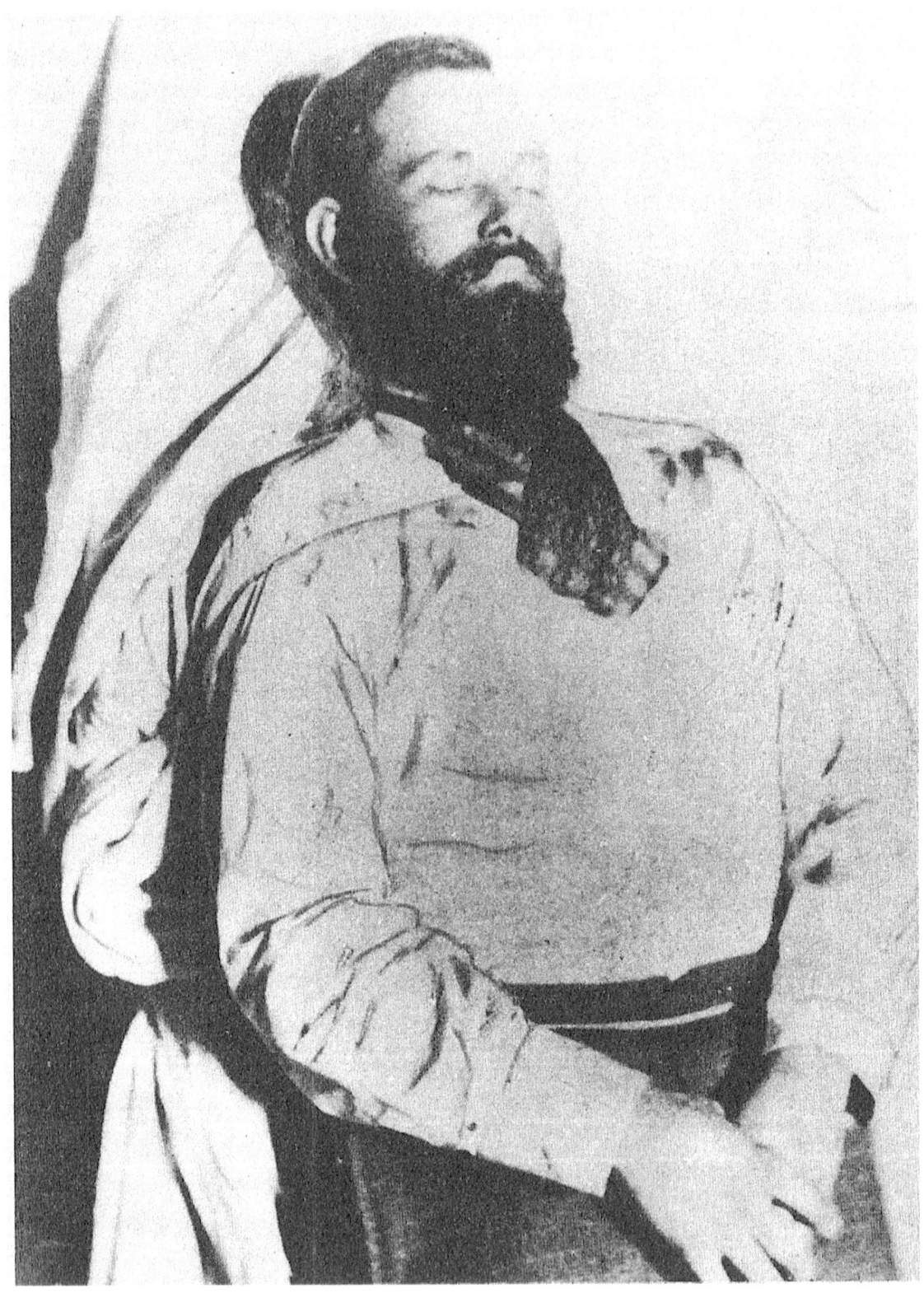

This is a photo of the dead body said to be Jesse James. Note blood on left shoulder, left arm, and bruises on top of right hand. Also, that his right hand is placed over his left hand so we can't see the missing finger tip on the middle finger on his left hand--which of course was just a coincidence to cover up the fact that the body belonged to someone else.

Jesse had a very high hairline, especially on the right side where he parted it.

Governor Crittenden of Missouri was a Southern sympathizer and an old friend of Jesse and Frank James. He worked with the Ford brothers to help pull off a hoax about Jesse's his death. Later, he gave Frank a full pardon.

Chapter Four

THE REST OF THE STORY—EXPOSING THE HOAX

Obviously, someone was shot, killed and buried in April of 1882, but there were many odd, secretive and mysterious circumstances associated with it that were unlike anything that had ever happened before, or anything like it since. And there have been questions about it for years as to who was really killed and buried.

We have been led to believe that it was Jesse James. It's been told in books, movies, in our history, and also in the old song: "That Dirty Little Coward That Shot Mr. Howard And Laid Poor Old Jesse In His Grave."

However, there have always been a number of people who refused to believe it and said they knew that Jesse had pulled off another hoax like he had tried before, but this time he had succeeded. Also, that Jesse was secretly hiding out someplace from the law.

There have always been adequate reasons to doubt Bob Ford's story that he had killed Jesse James, but now we have enough hard evidence to show that if he had killed somebody, it wasn't Jesse!

Even though that dramatic event occurred over a hundred years ago, it is still a matter of interest and investigation, and as a result, we have discovered some new physical evidence that has changed the idea that Jesse was killed.

DNA Evidence

The most surprising and most convincing evidence that it wasn't Jesse who was killed was discoverer in 1995 when there was a court order to exhume the body that was buried in Jesse's grave for DNA testing.

The DNA was to be compared with a man and his son in Oklahoma, who said that they were the great-grandson and the great-great grandson of Jesse's sister, Susan. They paid for the DNA to be done since they wanted to prove they were related to Jesse.

However, it turned out that the DNA was not a conclusive match. There was only a partial match to one of the men, but it didn't match any from the other man. The DNA should have matched with both men.

However, some people and some writers have interpreted the results differently and think that somehow it did match and therefore proved that it was

Jesse who was buried in the grave. There's been an open argument over it for a number of years

But to quote from "The Genetic Genealogist" report on the issue, in 2008, it reads: "Do the mtDNA results prove that the exhumed remains are those of Jesse James? The answer to this question must be no!"

So, some one else must be buried in Jesse's grave!

Then, another surprising bit of unexpected evidence was found during the testing that doesn't match up, a .38 caliber bullet was discovered in the skull! How could that be?

The Strange Bullet

At first, Bob Ford claimed he had used a .44 caliber revolver, then later claimed it was a .45 caliber. He even posed for a photograph of him holding a Colt .45 caliber revolver that he said he used--a gun that he said had been given to him by Jesse just a few days before, but that can not be substantiated.

But which was it? There is a big difference between a .38, a .44, and a .45.

That alone discredits Bob Ford's story that he had shot Jesse James—or perhaps he didn't shoot anybody!

Then, in addition to these discoveries, there have always been some other valid reasons to believe that the body in Jesse's grave is not Jesse's.

Photographic Evidence

One major example is by comparing photos of the person who was buried with photos of Jesse. It's easy to see that they are not of the same person and you don't need a magnifying glass to see the obviously big differences, especially in the hairlines.

Jesse had a noticeably receding hairline on both sides of his head--plus his hair was not thick. The photos of the dead man are quite different. He had a normal hairline that was lower and certainly was not receding on either side. His hair and beard were also much thicker and darker than Jesse's.

Since Jesse had a short beard at the time, it made it easier to pass off the dead man as Jesse because the dead man also had a beard. That was about the only thing they had in common, except that they were approximately of the same age and same size; but if their beards had been shaved off, more differences would have been seen.

Then, if you look carefully, there are some other differences around the ears and eyebrows. Also, Jesse had been described as having "well shaded eyes," meaning that they were rather deep set, but that is not seen in the photos of the dead person.

What more evidence is needed? That should be enough proof that it was not Jesse James--but there is still more evidence to consider.

Tintype Photos

At that time, all photos were tintypes, which were an original (one-of-a-kind) on a tin plate that could not be reproduced or copied until a few years later, in 1885, when George Eastman invented film photography. That made it possible to copy and print photos like we can today.

So, it worked to Jesse's advantage that the coroner did not compare the body to a photo of Jesse because he would have noticed the difference, and would known that Jesse was still alive. But that was unimportant anyway, since he was told by the Governor to identify the body as Jesse's.

Today, we can look at copies of the old tintypes and see for ourselves that the photos taken of the body are not that of Jesse James.

Interesting enough, in 1927, when a studio made thousands of copies of the tintype photo of the dead person and sent them out to the press, saying that it was Jesse James, they received many letters from the public, denying that the photo was of Jesse.

No Photos of Jesse's Body Scars

In the coroner's report, it mentioned a scar on the victim's right chest. It was commonly known that Jesse had been shot in that area during the Civil War and it had bothered him most of his life. But, was the scar really there on the corpse, or not? We don't know for sure because there weren't any photos of the body uncovered to show that they were actually there.

And what about the injury to the middle finger on Jesse's left hand? It was widely known that the tip of it was missing, either accidentally shot off when he was a kid, or had been chewed off in a fight. But notice in the several photos of the body, that the left hand is carefully placed over by his right hand so that it hides the tip of the finger…Of course, that just happened to be a coincidence!

A photo showing the injury on his left hand and the wound on his chest could have been convincing evidence that it was indeed, Jesse--but since they were not there on the dead man, they could not be photographed. That's the reason the photos of the body were taken with his shirt on in order to cover up the area where the chest wound would have been.

Obviously, those in charge of the body and of taking the photographs knew it wasn't Jesse and avoided taking photos that would show otherwise. Jesse had many important and loyal friends in the area who would, if given the chance, go along with the hoax and help persuade the coroner that the body was Jesse James. Jesse was considered a national hero by many who would gladly help in any way that they could.

In those days, it was quite common to take pictures of notorious criminals and bank robbers with their shirts off after they had been killed to show bullet wounds and other scars on the body. That happened to the Daltons, who were cousins to Jesse and to most of the others in the James-Younger gang. A look through some of the older books will show many photos of famous outlaws after they had been killed, especially the more famous ones—and Jesse was the most famous of all.

Some of the public got to wondering about the photos of the body and why they didn't show the serious chest wound, or the missing fingertip. That could have been convincing evidence that it was Jesse; but none were ever shown. Those were good questions and some answers were needed.

That led to a feeble attempt a few years later to take care of those questions when some dots were placed on one of the photographs of the body, supposedly to show the locations where Jesse had been shot. Then they were printed in some publications for the public to see, but it did little to change people's minds.

The Coroner's Predicament

For two days, the body was in the coroner's office while the coroner was busy trying to positively identify the body. The coroner had never met Jesse, so he didn't know what Jesse looked like.

All he had to go on was that the Ford brothers, Jesse's family and a few friends had claimed that it was Jesse, though there were some others who expressed their doubts. In fact, rumors were rapidly spreading among the public and in some of the newspapers that it was not Jesse who had been killed, but was someone else, and they could prove it. So, the coroner became hesitant, and wanted to make sure.

That was before finger printing was used, and also before photos could be copied and reproduced—only sketches carved on wooden blocks or similar materials could be printed. They were called "cuts" and were only as accurate as the skill of the artist.

However, the coroner could have compared the dead person to a tintype photo of Jesse if some one would have shown him one--but there is no record that anybody did, and that was probably on purpose because the coroner would have noticed the difference and known that the body was not Jesse James. Besides, not many pictures of Jesse had ever been taken, so there might not have been any available there at the time.

The Governor's Connection

There is little doubt that if the Governor hadn't unexpectedly stepped in on the second day after the shooting while the coroner was still trying to determine who the dead person was and officially announce that it was Jesse who had been killed, and that it was his body there in the morgue, the hoax would have soon been exposed and history would have known the truth.

But with the Governor's sudden announcement, that ended the inquest and made it "official" that it was Jesse's body there in the morgue. Then the body was guarded and quickly buried in his mother's yard in Kearney, Missouri.

After all, if the Governor proclaimed that the body in the morgue was Jesse's, that was good enough to make it official and accepted by history--although the Governor never went to the coroner's office to see for himself that it was Jesse's body!

But why would the Governor get involved? That was quite unexpected and quite extraordinary for a Governor to speak out in a case like that! What interest did he have in the situation?

Actually, he had some very good reasons for doing what he did, and they are most interesting. He had promised that if elected, he would put an end to the James gang. But after more than two years in office, Jesse had been very elusive and it looked like that was not going to happen. So, the Governor was faced with a dilemma and some hard decisions to make. So, here was his chance. It was a desperate plan, but also was his last chance.

He knew that if the hoax was discovered and it was found out that an innocent man had been murdered instead of Jesse, it would have exposed his part in it. That would have been more than just embarrassing to him. So, he needed to protect himself, and also the Ford brothers.

Who Was Killed Instead Of Jesse

It's obvious that someone else was killed and the body substituted for Jesse. As to who it was, we cannot be certain, but a few years ago some researchers and historians came up with the name of Charlie Bigelow. Of course, that might not have been his real name either, since many around Jesse used an alias: including Bob Ford who sometimes used the name of Jackson and also of Johnson.

Charlie Bigelow

Bigelow was thought to be a part-time member of Jesse's gang who had also pulled off some robberies on his own, then blamed them on Jesse. It was known how upset Jesse would get when he was blamed for robberies he did not commit. That would have been enough reason for Jesse to want him killed—or better yet, if Jesse thought he could substitute Charlie's body for his own as part of a hoax.

It was not uncommon for Jesse to kill members, or former members of his gang, to keep them quiet, or if they did something he didn't like, or other people he wanted to get rid of.

Actually, Jesse had just killed Ed Miller, an old member of his gang who had been working on his own and had pulled off a few robberies that he blamed on Jesse, so Jesse would not have hesitated to kill Charlie Bigelow for the some reason.

Jesse had tried to pull off a hoax about three years before that had failed because no dead body was ever found. Now, he was trying it again, but he needed a dead body to make it work. So, he made sure that one could be found this time, even if he had to kill the person himself!

No doubt, Jesse had been thinking about how he could escape from the law for a considerable length of time. He knew that if he didn't, sooner or later his luck would run out and he would be killed or captured, so he worked out a plan that involved the two Ford brothers. They agreed to it and saw where they could receive the huge reward money, and also become national heroes.

But it was necessary to find some one whose dead body could be passed off as Jesse's. It's interesting to wonder how long it took to find someone who resembled Jesse enough to make the plan work—especially if it was someone Jesse might have killed anyway. That would have made it especially convenient!

With the victim in the shed that morning with Jesse and the Ford brothers, that would have been the perfect set-up to kill him, then drag his body into the house while Jesse did a quick disappearing act. Then Bob fired a shot into the wall to attract attention and Jesse's wife ran into to room to see a body lying on the floor that was still bleeding.

The killing may have happened on the spur-of-the-moment and before Bob had a chance to think about what he was going to say. That explains his illogical and strange stories at the time. Apparently, he was making them up as he went along before he had time to think them through!

The Bullet In The Wall

It was the bullet that Bob fired into the wall to attract attention that souvenir hunters had tried to dig out, but apparently never succeeded. Otherwise, there is no explanation of where that bullet had come from because the bullet that killed the victim was still lodged in the head, and according to all reports, only one shot was heard--not two.

Do The Photos Give Away A Secret

There is also something quite interesting in the photo of the body—showing signs of some violence other than being shot in the head, because there is a lot a of noticeable blood stains on the left shoulder and near the elbow of the shirt, also some noticeable dark spots on his right hand, showing signs of bruising as if there had been a struggle and a gun had been forced out of his hand!

It's a bit difficult to understand how they could be there under the circumstances described by Bob. Had the man put up a fight for his life? It looks like he had, but was overcome. Otherwise, there is no other explanation to account for them. Take a look at the photo of the body and you can see that for yourself.

Maybe that person had tried to kill Jesse in the stable that morning so he could collect the reward money. But when he reached for his revolver (a .38 caliber) a struggle ensued, he was disarmed and shot with his own gun--maybe by Jesse himself.

Or if the victim realized that he was going to be shot, he drew his revolver to defend himself, but it was taken from him and shot with his own gun. Then his body dragged into the house.

That accounts for the .38 caliber bullet that was found in the body when it was exhumed in 1995, instead of the .44 or .45 caliber bullet that Bob claimed to have used.

In the coroner's report, it stated that the bullet had lodged inside the head just behind the left ear, so it didn't pass on through and enter the wall. That means the bullet was not powerful enough to pass through the skull—such as a .38 caliber bullet.

The bullet hole in the wall is rarely mentioned because it doesn't fit with Bob Ford's explanation of what happened, so it has usually been ignored as if it wasn't there—but it was there and most likely fired by Bob Ford to start the hoax routine and to cover up that the body had already been killed in the stable.

Jesse's First Hoax Attempt

What most people don't know, and what history has almost forgotten, is that there had been an earlier attempt by Jesse to pull off a hoax involving his death so that he could escape from the law. But there was a great deal of differences between the two incidents. The first one had happened about three years before, and didn't get much attention or publicity—and a dead body was not found!

George Shepherd Claimed He Had Killed Jesse

That first one had occurred when George W. Shepherd, an old friend of Jesse's who had been a former Confederate guerrilla fighter with him, but had turned bank robber, claimed that he had been on bad terms with Jesse and had killed him in order to collect the reward money.

He said that he had shot Jesse just after the Glendale train robbery in Joplin, Missouri in 1879 when he was member of the James gang. He claimed that he had buried the body somewhere in Clay County. He even had a physician's certificate of death on Jesse, and Jesses' mother said that she thought he son was dead in order to put people off the track, but authorities could never find the body nor could they find Jesse because he and his family had quietly moved on to another town and were living there under an assumed name.

Was A Put-Up Job

After several years of investigation and during a period while Jesse was being quiet, Shepherd finally admitted that: "It was all a put-up job with the James brothers, so Jesse could escape from the law, and I would no more shoot Jesse than I would my own brother."

Then, after he heard about the second hoax, he was one of the first to speak out publicly with doubts that Jesse had really been killed.

It's also interesting to note that Shepherd later remarked that he was completely disillusioned with the public, since the "Kansas City Times" had not only called him a "Judas Iscariot", but he had received more abuse than Jesse ever had. Jesse had many admires and supporters in that area.

Jesse's first hoax attempt was reported in some of the newspapers at the time. Also, it has been documented in several books on Jesse James, including at least two biographies on him: "The Saga Of Jesse James" by Carl W. Breihan; and in "The Outlaws" by James D. Horan. Both Breihan and Horan are recognized as the most prominent biographers of Jesse James. So, the idea of trying another hoax was obviously not new for Jesse and anyone can still read the story for themselves in those publications, plus some others.

Jesse Was A Clever Person

Jesse was known as a shrewd and clever person and he realized the importance of publicity. He had not forgotten about the first hoax that almost worked and he was looking for an opportunity to try it again, but he needed to get more people involved to attract more attention and publicity, plus some excitement, such as the shot that Bob Ford had fired inside his house.

He knew that under the circumstance that if he didn't think of something, someone would sooner or later be tempted by the huge reward and would shoot him. He knew that he had to do something to change the situation soon—and he did!

We can understand that Jesse wanted to do a better job the next time and to be sure that a body could be found—but not his!

So, the probability that Jesse was trying another hoax was thought by many people as the most likely—especially after hearing the dubious story of how Bob Ford claimed to have killed him, plus some of the strange things that didn't add up.

Many Doubts Reported

In addition to George W. Shepherd and a few others who told reporters that they doubted that Jesse had really been killed, was Joseph O. Shelby. He was a very prominent figure and big landowner in the area. He was known as the only Confederate general who had never surrendered. He also had been a friend of the James brothers and had supported them in the past.

When asked by a newspaper editor to write an obituary for Jesse, he instead sent a letter of warning to the editor that he would not do that. He said it was "Because it is very possible that Jesse is still alive, and that the affair in St. Joseph was prearranged and done by parties who seek to obtain the great reward offered for the bold raider, dead or alive!"

Chicago Newspaper Reports Jesse Not Killed

Then, just two days after Bob Ford claimed he had killed Jesse James, a special article appeared on the front page of the "Chicago Times" that was written by one of their correspondents. The article said that the correspondent had just been told in St Louis that Jesse James was not dead and that there were men in the city who were willing to bet money on it.

The article also went on to say that the correspondent had just talked to some prominent individuals in the area who agreed that Jesse was not dead, and when asked what the identification of the body by his own mother meant, they shrugged their shoulders and said, "Well, you wait and see!"

Then, when they were asked what object Ford would have in killing an innocent man, he was told: "Ford gets money and immunity, and Governor Crittenden thinks he has satisfied the people and made a point."

Another prominent man by the name of Bacon, said that the Governor will get more money out of it than anybody else.

When asked what the stories from Jesse's widow meant, they said that she had been posted and was playing her part well. They also said that the action of the Governor in the matter will show him up in a very "reprehensible light".

That prediction proved to be very true. When Crittenden ran for re-election, he was defeated. Then later, when he was nominated for a foreign post, President Cleveland turned him down. The President said that he did that because "Crittenden had bargained with the Fords for the killing of Jesse James."

The Reward Money

Then, there is something very curious about who received the reward money. It had been promised to Bob and Charles by the Governor, but they only received a portion of it—not the entire amount. Though the Governor never said exactly what they received, he admitted that he had to give a lot of it to other people who were involved, including the local sheriff and others in the legal departments, but he failed to say who got what.

However, he was quoted as saying: "I paid out twenty thousand dollars in rewards to various persons for the capture and overthrow of this band of desperadoes. Not one dollar of which was taken from the State Treasury."

Of course, that's understandable because a number of other people had to be involved to make the scheme work, though he never said who they were or what they did.

From his statements, it proves that others were involved in the scheme. If Bob and his brother alone had shot Jesse themselves, as they claimed, and immediately went to the city jail and gave themselves up—who else was involved?

If not, then why would other unnamed people be paid reward money? If it wasn't a "pay-off" to others who helped in the scheme, what else could it have been? It also proves that there were other people involved than just Bob and Charles Ford.

Texas Attorney General Also Claims It Was a Hoax

The question of whether Jesse James had really been killed by Bob Ford, or not, has never gone away. It has always been a topic of interest and mystery.

In 1997, as the result of an investigation into the incident, the former Texas Attorney General, Waggner Carr, wrote an article in which he said that he had proof that Jesse had not been killed.

He said that the story of Jesse James being killed was a big hoax and he could prove it.

He explained that he had once been hired by some relatives of Jesse James to represent them in court in case they found some gold that Jesse had buried near Waco, Texas as part of a KGC treasure.

Carr said that he found the story interesting, but if he was going to defend them in court, he would need more information. So they supplied him with literally thousands of documents, including photographs, personal family letters, newspaper articles, audio tapes, and other material. Some of it included affidavits signed by people who were dead by then, but who claimed they had known Jesse, that he was not killed by Bob Ford, and that he had lived on for years in a secret life.

Jesse's' Secret Meeting With The Governor

The article went on to say that since Jesse wanted to get rid of Charles Bigelow and that Governor Crittendon wanted to get rid of Jesse, Jesse arranged a secret meeting with the Governor to work out the situation. It was known that Jesse had contributed money to his campaign funds and that they had been on friendly terms. There is also a record that Jesse had once hired him to act as his attorney, and its also been thought that they were distantly related.

The article described the meeting as being held in the forest one night between Jesse and the Governor. Jesse had three of his friends hiding nearby so that they could see and hear the conversation. Among the audio tapes that Carr said he heard was a copy of an early CBC Radio Show in which all three of the men were interviewed, and each told the story in which the Governor agreed to allow Jesse to kill Bigelow, bury him as Jesse James, then Jesse would secretly leave Missouri, take up a new name, and stay in hiding.

To live in hiding at that time would not have been difficult to do. That was long before Social Security numbers, telephones or telephone directories, and before driver's licenses. Most anyone could live about anywhere under a false name, and many people did.

Carr concluded by saying that there was also reason to believe that J. Frank Dalton, the old man who showed up in Lawton, Oklahoma in 1948 and said that he was the real Jesse James and who later died in Texas in 1951, could have really been Jesse James!

J. Frank Dalton

In addition to the Attorney General's statement about J. Frank Dalton, we are finding out now that there is some convincing evidence that the old man really was Jesse James-- though not all historians agree.

But still, there are the testimonials from many reliable people who met the old man and positively identified him as Jesse James, saying that he answered questions that only the real Jesse James would have known, and also that he had the physical resemblance to Jesse. He was about of the same physical build, bone structure, facial resemblance, a high hairline, and with piercing blue eyes.

Then, there is the surprising results from the coroner's report that was held at the Estes Funeral Home in Granbury, Texas on 17 August 1951 after the old man had died there and was buried in a borrowed grave. Witnessing the examination were Sheriff Oran C. Baker, Joe L. Deering, Harley Cheery, Mack L. Likers, and E B. Price who was the local Justice of the Peace at Granbury.

The results were most astonishing!

The examination showed:

He was an aged man about 5 feet 8 and 1/2 inches tall.
His eyes were blue and had fair skin.
Two bullet wounds in right side of chest near nipple.
Bullet wound on lower left side of stomach.
Bullet wound along right side near second lower rib
Bullet wound though the left shoulder.
Bullet wound on right side of neck.
Two bullet wounds on right shoulder.
Three or four bullet wounds along left arm from wrist to elbow.
Three or four bullet wounds above elbow on left arm.
Evidence of numerous bullet wounds up and down right arm.
Bullet wound between shoulders at base of neck.
Bullet wound along the hairline above both eyes.
Bullet wound under right eye causing eye to droop.
Evidence of about 8 or 10 bullet wounds up and down right arm.
Tip end sort of "chewed" off on end of left index finger.
Evidence of rope burns on his neck.
Both feet showed evidence of having been severely burned, plus scars on both knees.
Bad wound on back between both of his hips.
Cataracts in both eyes.
Powder burns across chin that were hidden by a Buffalo Bill type goatee.
(A total of 32 bullet wounds from his forehead to his knees)

It positively proved that he had lived an incredibly dangerous life, and most of it matched with what was known about some of Jesse's injuries—especially the damage to the tip of his left index finger, the bullet wound on the right side of his chest, the rope burns around his neck, and burned scars on his feet caused by Union Soldiers when they tried to make him tell where his brother Frank was hiding. So, if he wasn't Jesse James--then who could he possible be?

Interestingly enough, he commented on the bullet hole in the wall that souvenir hunters had tried to dig out. While being interviewed, he was asked about that famous morning's events. He said that he had been hiding in the shed and when he heard the shot in the house, he knew that his plan had worked.

So, if he really was Jesse James who had lived out most of his life afterwards without being discovered, then apparently he didn't live peaceably and quietly as has been assumed.

Of course, that's not positive proof that he was Jesse James, but it is certainly possible, and he did convince many people that he was.

However, some writers and historians have also claimed that there was another person who could have been Jesse James later in life. He went under the name of James L. Courtney and appeared in a few old group photographs. His appearance does show a similarity to Jesse. So, there are at least two possibilities, or more, to indicate that Jesse had pulled off a hoax.

Some Outlaws Lived With Many Bullet Wounds

Since shotguns were often used in gunfights back then, some of J. Frank Daltons' bullet scars could have been from shotgun pellets. It's hard to believe that someone could have survived that many wounds from rifle or pistol bullets. The same goes for Cole Younger who often rode with the James gang. When he died, he still had 17 bullets in his body.

The bullet wounds on J. Frank Dalton and the 17 bullets still in Cole Younger's body when he died, does seem unbelievable, but there were other outlaws back then who lived to a ripe old age after being shot many times.

Texas Jack

The notorious Nathaniel Reed, better known under his nickname as "Texas Jack," who had ridden with the Dalton gang, Bill Doolin, Henry and Belle Starr, had been shot 27 times; and when he died at age of 87 in Tulsa, Oklahoma in 1950, he still had 14 bullets in his body. Obviously, some men at that time were incredibly tough. He had reformed and had spent his last few years as an evangelist.

Strange Photo of Bob Ford

Included in this book is an often shown photo of Bob Ford that was taken in a photo gallery some time after he supposedly shot Jesse James. It shows a very carefully posed photo of Bob Ford in which he is sending a subtle, but clear signal that he did not kill Jesse James.

When you look at the photo, notice that he has taken the trouble to wrap a dark cloth around his right leg; that his right leg is also resting on a step so that it is higher and more noticeable than his left leg; that his right hand had been placed on top of his right leg to make it more noticeable and to show that his trigger finger is crossed with another finger; that he is holding the gun in his left hand instead of his right; and that the gun is pointing in the direction of his crossed fingers.

For this publication, the area of his right hand has been enlarged to show that he has purposely crossed his fingers. That has gone unnoticed before and not commented on since the original photo has usually been trimmed down or shown in a much smaller size.

I believe that Bob was caught in a predicament and his conscious was bothering him. He had been described several times as a nice young man, but he had taken a lot of abuse and didn't like being called a villain when he knew he wasn't; and he didn't want to forever be known as "That dirty little coward that shot Mr. Howard," so he devised a clever way to signal with crossed fingers over his gun to show he hadn't.

He couldn't say directly at the time that he had not killed Jesse because that would undo the work and planning they had done to make the hoax work. Also, he and his brother would have to give the reward money back and probably face charges of fraud and of murdering an innocent man, so he devised a clever way to try to show his innocence.

Otherwise, why would he pose for a photo like this—wrap a dark cover around his right leg (maybe to keep it warm)—then hold it higher than his left leg (for some unknown reason)—cross the trigger finger on his right hand with another finger (because he had crooked fingers)—and he is holding the gun in his left hand instead of his right--(he forgot that he was right-handed). No! I really don't think so!

The Real Secret Of Frank and Jesse James

Also, it is most interesting to consider the remarks that were made by Frank James's wife, Ann, who was often quoted in the newspapers for saying, "The Real Secret of Frank and Jesse James would die with her."

When she died in 1944 at the age of 91, it made the headlines of several newspapers: "James Vow is Kept, Outlaw's Widow Dies Without Telling Secrets, She Was Loyal To The End."'

There has been much speculation over the years as what it was that she wasn't telling, how important it was, why she wouldn't tell it, and if known, how it would have changed the story of Frank and Jesse James.

Obviously, there is more to the story than what history has told, and perhaps we will never know what it was—or do we?

I believe that her secret was that Jesse had not been killed as reported, but had escaped from the law and secretly lived on, and sometimes paid secret visits to his wife, his mother, and to his brother, Frank. It was not like Jesse to never see them again—but it was something that Ann could not reveal.

Bob And Charles Never Hid Out

One more thing to consider that also casts further doubt on Bob Ford's story of killing Jesse James is that he never went into hiding or ever seemed to have feared for his life afterwards as many people thought he would, although he was killed four years later in Colorado by someone he had an argument with; but some historians believe it could have been in revenge for killing Jesse.

Instead of hiding out as expected, Bob and his brother made public appearances by going on stage to tell and re-enact the event—even bragging about it.

In those days, revenge killings were rather common, and for far less reasons than what Bob was accused of. Jesse had many loyal friends, plus his brother, Frank, who I'm sure that some of them would have tried it--unless they knew differently!

A reporter once wrote: "If Frank James had been the right kind of man, he would have avenged the death of his brother, Jesse. He would have never rested until he had killed Bob and Charles Ford."

If the Ford brothers had killed Frank James, you can bet your life that Jesse would have killed them.

Several years later, after Frank had surrendered and been pardoned by the Governor, he told some reporters that he didn't have any hatred against Bob Ford for killing Jesse. He said that he understood because the temptation of the reward money was too much for him to resist.

Of course, Frank didn't ever intend to kill Bob and that's because he knew that Jesse was still alive and that Bob had actually helped Jesse escape from the law.

Jesse's Epitaph

Then, there is also a rather strange epitaph that Jesse's mother wrote for Jesses's grave: "In Loving Memory of My Beloved Son, Murdered By a Traitor and Coward Whose Name is Not Worthy To Appear Here."

She was noted for having a sharp tongue and for speaking out, especially to criticize. She never hesitated to say whatever she had in mind, so why didn't she mention Bob Ford's name? Was that because she knew that Bob Ford hadn't killed him?

Afterwards

Actually, there are many more reason to believe that Bob Ford did not kill Jesse James than there are reasons to believe that he did; and when we take a careful look at the historical facts, no other logical conclusion can be made, other than it was a gigantic hoax that was perpetuated on the American people and an innocent man was murdered instead of Jesse.

Of course, Jesse did not pull off this hoax by himself, and he was not the only one who profited from it. For him, it was a way of saving his life and escaping from the law. For the Governor, it was to his advantage to keep his campaign promise of doing away with Jesse and his gang. And for the Ford brothers, they could profit from it financially and also become heroes and celebrities with a place in history.

Additionally, there was also a profit in it for the various other officials that the Governor admitted giving some of the reward money to for assisting in the situation. So, it was teamwork by a number of individuals.

A Peace Treaty

Some people believed, and it has been commented on by several of Jesse's biographers, that what really happen with Jesse was that it was basically more like a peace treaty that had been worked out. That was because Jesse had been a big embarrassment to the law for over 15 years and there seemed to be no way of stopping him, especially after the brazen and deadly Northfield Bank robbery. After that, there were growing demands from the public, many law enforcement officers and some politicians, to put an end to Jesse and his lawlessness--one way or another!

So, if something could be worked out whereby it would be thought that Jesse had been killed for his crimes, but had actually agreed to disappear and live quietly and peaceable somewhere else, like in Tennessee where his brother was, that would be a win-win situation all the way around, especially for Jesse. For him, that would be a much better alternative than being hunted the rest of his life and eventually being killed or captured, and I believe there is much credence to that story.

The passage of time often solves questions of the past, and now we have evidence that someone else was killed, rather than Jesse!

History deserves to know the truth!

LEGENDS

Skeleton may 'lve.tobe *1*. n0s outlai

Researchers to test DNA in effort to verify *if* grave is Jesse James'

By Amy Ugnltz
AssociATED PREss

KEARNEY.Mo..-Most of the upper skeleton of the man buried Wlder Jesse James' headstone was recovered today by researchers out to determine whether the legendary outlaw is actually buried in that grave.

Most of the skull, the upper rib cage and both arms were recovered along with some teeth that would be useful in DNA testing.

"It looks very promising with respect to DNA," said James E. Starrs, the scientist leading the project.

Metal casket handles found in the plot turned out to be solid silver, providing more evidence that the grave was that of James, or at least that of the man buried under James' name more than a century ago.

"There's nothing to discount it and everything to support it," Starrs said

Starrs, a professor of forensic science and law at George Washington University, wants to compare DNA samples with DNA

TWO WORKERS at Mount Olivet Cemetery in Kearney, Mo., dig up the grave purported to hold the remains of outlaw Jesse James on Monday.
ASSOCIATED PRESS·

of people confirmed to be James' descendants. Teeth often give better DNA samples because they take longer to deteriorate, researchers have said;

The exhumation is aimed at settling numerous questions about James, chiefly whether the bones are really his.

Some people claim the body beneath the Jesse James headstone is not his. They say

the robber of trains and banks did not die when he was shot in the head in 1882 at his St. Joseph home, that instead MI aked his death and had more children. Among those claiming to be descended from James are the wife of one exhumation team member and even Starrs' own daughter-in-law.

The DNA question should be answered by mid-September, Starrs said.

Who's Grave Is This? This article appeared in the "Pasadena Tribune" Newspaper on 19 July 1995 (From the author's collection.)

This is a very carefully posed photo of Bob Ford in which he is sending a clear, but subtle, message that he did not kill Jesse James. Note the elevated right leg with a dark cover over it to make it more noticeable that he has his 'trigger finger' crossed with another finger. Also, he is holding the gun in his 'left' hand instead of his right, and he has it pointing almost directly to his crossed fingers. How much more obvious could it be?

Chapter Five

THE FORD BROTHERS ON TRIAL

False Confessions

The trial of the Ford brothers who were charged with the murder of Jesse James was one of the most unusual trials ever held in this country. For one thing, it was a trial for a murder that they had not committed and they knew it, but they had voluntarily turned themselves in and pleaded guilty in hopes of collecting the huge reward money. Also, it was their chance to become rich and famous.

To voluntarily plead guilty to a murder is very risky under any circumstances--even to one you didn't commit. But the Fords had the support of the Governor who had promised to give them the reward money and also to pardon them in case they went to trial and faced criminal charges.

The Secret Agreement With The Governor

It is a matter of record that before the shooting the Fords had met secretly with the Governor several times to work out what was described in the newspapers later as "Their plans to kill Jesse so they could collect the reward money."

It so happened that the Governor was agreeable with the plan to make it look like they had killed Jesse. It was subterfuge on a grand scale!

If it worked out, the Governor thought that it would help him out politically because he was being criticized by his political enemies for not doing away with Jesse and his gang like he had promised to do during his campaign promises, but Jesse was still on the loose and causing trouble.

The information on this secret agreement with the Fords was brought out and also confirmed during the trial as part of the testimony. It was rather surprising information, but the Governor never denied it, saying that under the circumstances, it was justified. However, he received much criticism over it later as some predicted that he would.

The Fords probably did not realize the precarious situation they were getting into. They had not expected to go on trial, or if they did, they thought the charges would be dismissed as justifiable homicide--but that didn't happen. They were found guilty of murder-in-the-first-degree and unexpectedly were sentenced to be hanged!

After all, they had rather brazenly confessed and told the court how they had done it—cowardly details and all. The guilty verdict was unanimously reached on the following day; but the Governor intervened two hours later by sending a telegram to the court in which he pardoned them both. With that, the trial and the charges were quickly over, the body had already been buried, the brothers went free, and the truth was covered up and hidden from history for many years.

The Brothers Had Been Lucky

It should be noted that the brothers had been very lucky with the way things turned out because their trial had been on false confessions and fake information from the start. On the first day of the trial, they had pleaded guilty but never entered a defense. They wanted to get the trial over quickly before something came up to expose their confessions as a fraud. If it had dragged on for a while, it could have easily fallen apart and the truth could have come out, so it was a quick trial and over in just two days.

Whether they had realized it or not, the Fords had put themselves in a very dangerous position for a number of reasons. Not the least of which would have been chances of being assassinated by someone in revenge for killing Jesse who was a national hero to many and who some had called 'America's Robin Hood'.

Their part in the hoax had been a rather bold and courageous act, as well as by the Governor and the others who were involved because it had been very risky. Numerous things could have easily gone wrong that would have changed the outcome, like if it been discovered that the body wasn't Jesse's, or if Jesse had been discovered still alive someplace, or if the hoax had been exposed for the deception that it was.

If so, it would have been a scandal of major proportions with serious consequences for all involved, including, no doubt, charges of impeachment against the governor, or even worse.

Since there had been no timetable or specific date set for when the killing was supposed to take place, it could have been months before the opportunity came up to shoot Charlie Bigelow, or whoever the victim was!

Obviously, something could have easily happened between the time the Governor made his promise and when the Fords went to trial that could have easily changed the situation. If they hadn't received his pardon when they did, things would have ended much differently, especially for the Fords.

For instance, what if the Governor had a sudden heart attack, or suffered a critical illness—or worse yet, what if he had suddenly died; or maybe changed his mind, or was unable to pardon them for some reason. Or, he could have decided that it was best not to get involved in something like this after all. Actually, he was severely criticized for what he did and he suffered politically for it later as some people said he would.

So, whether they realized it or not, the lives of the Ford brothers had been hanging on a rather thin thread. It was only because the Governor came through with his promise when he did were they able to avoid the death sentence.

The Hoax

After the shooting, there had been a need to get the coroner to quickly identify the body as Jesse's and to get the body buried as soon as possible before it was discovered that it wasn't Jesse, as some people suspected.

It should be remembered that while the coroner was trying to identify the body, the Governor sent a telegram to him on the following day, saying that it was Jesse who had been killed and that the body there in the morgue was Jesse's--even though he never went there to see for himself!

That officially ended the investigation and the body was immediately shipped off for burial. That relieved the pressure off of it being discovered that the body was not Jesse's.

The success of the hoax had depended upon the cooperation of a number of other people in addition to the Governor. It had been like a big stage play with everybody doing their part at the right time. That included the Governor, Jesse's family and friends, Sheriff Timberlake from Clay Country, and also the sheriff's associates who carefully guarded the body as they escorted it to his mother's home for burial to make sure nobody examined it to discover that it was not Jesse inside the casket.

But some of the public was still reluctant to believe that Jesse had really been killed. There were some lingering questions and some strong suspicions among many of them, and also with some newspaper reporters that Jesse was still alive; and that this was another hoax to deceive the public into believing that he had been killed.

They had good reasons to believe that because of the many strange and unexplainable events that had happened. Also, the stories that Bob and Charles had told about how they had killed Jesse were just too implausible to be true and many people and some historians throughout the years have believed that Jesse had not been killed—and now, many people agree with them.

It's clear that the Fords had never intended to kill Jesse, but to make it look like they had. To kill Jesse himself would have been very dangerous to attempt, so better if someone else could be killed and make it look like it had been Jesse.

It is naive to think that the Ford brothers thought up this cleaver plan themselves and how to carry it out, because it would, and did, require the cooperation of Jesse's family and many friends, plus some officials, including the Governor, to make it work.

Who else could have planned and arranged this hoax but Jesse? Actually, this was and his second hoax. He had tried another hoax two years before in an attempt to escape from the law that most everyone knew about. It almost worked, and it did for about a year before it was found to be a hoax. But Jesse wanted to do a more convincing job this time, so he enlisted the help of the Ford brothers and numerous others. Jesse had many friends and some strong supporters.

Since Jesse and the Governor had been old friends, there is good reason to believe that Jesse had also met secretly with the Governor to work out the hoax. In fact, Waggner Carr, the former Texas Attorney General, said he had proof that they had--and it only makes sense that they did.

The key to the successful ending of the hoax had been that the Governor had kept his promise and pardoned the Ford brothers when he did. That put a quick end to all charges against them and they were free.

Otherwise, more would have happened and it would have ended differently—most likely with the execution of the Fords!

For one thing, they had not planned on defending themselves. They had been too pre-occupied with convincing the jury that they had succeeded in killing Jesse, then depending on the Governor to protect them with his pass to get out of jail, free!

A Quick Change Of Pleas

However, if they hadn't received the pardon when they did, don't you think they would have quickly changed their stories to claim they were not guilty and would have said most anything, especially the truth, to save themselves from being hanged?

You know they would, regardless of who they incriminated, and that would have been from the Governor on down. That could have set off a chain of surprising events, plus a scandal of major proportions that would have changed that part of our history.

The Governor could have been impeached, or resigned, other officials would have a lot of explaining to do, Jesse would have been on the run again, the Fords would have received a lot of criticism, none of the reward money, and probably would have been executed in the end for killing an innocent person!

Though it really didn't happen, it's intriguing to see how easily it could have if something had gone wrong with the daring scheme and it hadn't worked out as planned, or if it had been exposed as a hoax, or if the Governor hadn't kept his promise to come through with the pardon when he did.

Defending Themselves

Otherwise, the Fords would have been left on their own to defend themselves against the death sentence and to deny that they had killed Jesse.

Of course, their first reaction, would be to claim that it had all been a hoax—a set-up to make it look like they had killed Jesse so they could receive the reward and Jesse could escape from the law, and that he was still alive and hiding out someplace. Therefore, they were innocent of the charges.

We don't know if their attorney was good or not, but lets assume in this hypothetical case that he could have risen to the occasion and could have filed for a new trial in order to get their death sentence changed. If so, some most interesting events would have occurred.

But would a new trial have been a way out for them? Where would it lead too? That's interesting to consider because if somehow they could have convinced a new judge or a jury that they had not killed Jesse, then some questions and other problems would have quickly come up that would have not only put them on the defensive again, but in an even more threatening and difficult position than before--like jumping from the frying pan into the fire, and they would be accused of murder again, but this time for murdering somebody else—the man who had been buried in Jesse's grave.

For sure, someone had been shot, killed and buried! There was no denying that. So, if it wasn't Jesse, then it was someone else--an innocent man, and someone guilty of that. And who else could have done it except them because they had admitted to shooting the man who had been buried. That would have placed them in a situation with hardy any way out.

Under cross-examination, how would their stories hold up? Obviously, not believable! And the more they talked, the less likely they would be believed, but what other choice would they have? At this point, their situation would have been desperate.

For them, it would have been like double Jeopardy—getting out of one bad situation, but getting into another because if they had somehow succeeded in getting a new trial, then they would soon have to defend themselves against new charges of killing someone else--the victim. And what do you think their chance would be of getting out of that, especially if they claimed that it was Jesse himself who had done the killing?

Not likely at all!

A New Trial

Trying to convince a new judge or a jury that another man had been with them in the stable that morning, that Jesse himself killed the man after a struggle, then they dragged the body into the house, still bleeding, Bob fired a shot into the wall, Jesse suddenly left, then they claimed that the body was Jesse's so they could claim the reward, wouldn't have much chance of success.

Who would have believed that or most anything else they might have said later? It appeared that they had killed an innocent man in cold blood in order to get the reward money. After that, nobody would have any sympathy for them.

Guilty Or Not

If you had been a judge or a member of a jury in a retrial and heard the brother's claim that they had not killed Jesse or anybody else because it had all been a hoax so that Jesse could escaped from the law--that it had been a set-up involving the Governor who had promised to give them the reward money and also a pardon in case they were found guilty, but because he had not kept his promise they were to be hanged for killing Jesse! And now they are claiming that it was Jesse himself, not them, who had killed the victim. It would be hard to believe!

It's interesting to contemplate that situation. Though it really didn't happen, it easily could have if the Governor had not come through with his pardon when he did--and what a story it would have been.

It would have led to the biggest murder mystery trial of the century. Actually, it would have been a double murder mystery because there would have been a big question as to who was killed, and also who killed him.

Come to thin k of it, it still is a mystery even today because we don't really know for sure who was killed, nor who did the killing because the evidence and logic does not support the old historical accounts.

The trial would have been spectacular and a great human-interest drama with the lives of two men at stake, plus the reputation of some high-level officials. The list of witnesses and defendants would have been large and impressive, including the Governor, the corner, the undertakers, local law enforcement officers, members of Jesse's family and friends, etc. It would have filled the courtroom for weeks, or maybe months. The charges, accusations and denials would have been sensational, especially with the Governor being involved in a more-or-less murder for hire!

The reporters and newspapers would have had a field day with it, filling the headlines and front pages of the newspapers for months. It would have read like a 'Who Done It Novel' and the outcome of the trial could have changed our history as well as deciding the guilt or innocence of the Ford brothers.

It could have easily become as famous, or even more so, than the historical "Scopes Monkey Trial" that occurred in 1925 over whether or not human evolution could be taught in public schools in Tennessee. It was that trial that pitted two of our country's most famous attorneys, William Jennings Bryan and Clarence Darrow, against each other.

Also, if there had been a second trial, perhaps they would have discovered then who was really killed instead of Jesse.

Who Was Killed

Historical writers and researches today have a big advantage over those in the past. With the Internet, research it is now much faster, more accurate and far more extensive than before. Subject items are easier to find and are loaded with much information from many old historical records and accounts that have been located, including some extensive genealogy records that were not available until recently. They have filled in some gaps and have answered many questions from the past as well as substantiating some event.

A Cousin That Resembled Jesse

This has led some researchers and historians to some new formation and conclusions about who was killed, as well as some of the circumstances. They have reason to believe, and some have documented it, that it was a cousin of Jesse's on his father's side who was killed, though they can't be sure of which one he was. But this cousin had often rode with the gang and also looked a lot like Jesse, especially since they both had beards and both were about the same age and about the same size; so it would have often been difficult to tell them apart. Also, he was around Jesse's home much of the time.

That's interesting information as well as being logical since it would easily explain how his body could have been passed off as Jesses, and also explain the similarity of the DNA test which was a close match, but not an exact match to some of Jesse's descendants.

We know that families often depended upon each other back then and often worked together, and that was especially true with the James. But the information also reveals that this cousin was spending too much time around

Jesse's home and becoming too familiar with Jesse's wife, who was quite attractive, and that Jesse became suspicious and decided to kill him.

It's a matter of record that it was not uncommon for Jesses to kill some of his own gang members, or others, if they did something he didn't like. Jesse had no compulsion against killing anyone for very little reason. He was a dangerous man!

The information that it was a cousin of Jesse's who was killed and that it was Jesse who assassinated him is considerable more believable and logical than the inconsistent and questionable stories that the Ford brothers had told.

Cousin Who Used The Name Of Howard

A short time ago, I had a call from a man who had bought some of my previous books on Jesse James and the Knights Of The Golden Circle. He is an experienced historian on Jesse and Frank James and is also is a County Historian in Kansas. His family extends far back into the States' history, and where some of them had been members of the KGC, including some who had served as sentinels to watch over some KGC treasure sites!

In our discussion, he revealed some little known and unpublished information that I happen to know was accurate...plus including the name of the man who had threatened to shoot my grandfather if he tried to change the fence line on our old farm in Kansas back in about 1928, that I had written about. It had been one of his great uncles, and I recognized the name as one the families who had lived in the area at that time.

He also said that according to some old records that he knew about, it was a cousin who had been killed, and that he had been using the name of Howard at the time.

That's interesting, and also would explain the famous old song: "That Dirty Little Coward That Shot Mr. Howard!

Historical records never had an accurate or complete list of Jesse's' gang members. That is because they were all outlaws, or part-time outlaws, and had to keep their identification and activities secret most of the time. Also, most of the time they used fictions names, many had beards, and they almost always wore masks during their robberies.

But history does record that some of Jesses' cousins were members of his gang, so that information fits in with this new disclosure. It also gives a more logical and believable explanation as to who was killed instead of Jesse, and also why; plus that his body would closely resembled Jesse's. It's like a missing piece from a jigsaw puzzle—it fits!

Wood Hite

One cousin of Jesse's who was often mentioned by name was Wood Hite. It was known that he frequently rode with Jesse, and some have reason now to believe that it was Hite that Jesse killed. But whether Hite ever went by the name of Howard, or not, has not been established.

However, there are some accounts of a gunfight between Wood Hite and Bob Ford in which he was killed by Bob—shot in the head! This supposedly happened in a room of a house where Bob Ford had stayed, and happened just a very short time before Bob Ford claimed he had killed Jesse.

That is interesting, because there was nobody else present to confirm the story, except Dick Liddel, an old-time member of Jesses' gang. He claimed that he had also pulled his gun and fired several shots at Wood Hite, but missed. Then, they hid the body. There are some confliction stories regarding that incident and also what happened to the body. One historian claims that there doesn't seem to be any record of his burial, or grave site, so we really don't know for sure if Wood Hite was killed then, or not—or if Wood Hite could have been killed later by Jesse, then buried in his grave.

However, curiously enough, one prominent book by Carl W. Breihan, who was perhaps the greatest biographer of Jesse and Frank James, briefly states that "Governor Crittenden had pardoned Bob Ford for the killing Wood Hite," but gives no further information.

That appears to be a little-known piece of history and I wondered why the Governor would have done that--or if it was an error, or maybe a mix-up of the records, or is there more to the story somewhere? Maybe it was Wood Hite's body that was buried in Jesse's grave?

Perhaps we will never know for sure who was buried in Jesses' grave. Obviously, the historical accounts have many credibility gaps and inconsistencies—including some stories and information that are absurd and - contrary to each other. They simply don't add up, especially when considering the different and conflicting stories that Bob Ford and his brother told at first, then changed some on the next day. Why?

At first, Bob said he was alone in the room with Jesse when he fired the shot. The next day, he claimed that Charles had also been in the room, and together, they both pulled their revolvers, but only he (Bob) fired the shot.

Bob also claimed he had used a .44 caliber revolver, but posed for a picture a few days later with a .45 caliber revolver that he claimed he had used—but a .38 caliber bullet was found in the skull of the body that was exhumed in 1995. Why?

According to the Genetic Genealogist Report, the DNA from the dead body was not a positive match to Jesses' relatives when it should have been. Why?

If Bob and Charles Ford had really worked out an agreement with the Governor to kill Jesse and were promised the $20,000 reward, then why did they only receive a portion of it?.

But perhaps the most unbelievable story that Bob Ford told was that Jesse had taken off all of his guns and deliberately laid them on the bed in front of them, then turned his back and stood on a stool to straighten up a picture above the door-way. That is about as believable as saying that John Dillinger took his guns off before he went to rob a bank! Bob should have come up with some better stories than what he told!

Also, Jesse had tried a hoax about his death a few years before that almost succeeded, so why not believe that he wouldn't try it again? The Attorney General of Texas certainly thought so, and he said he had proof that he had, so coming from a person like him, there must something to it.

From the start, there have always been a number of people, especially those who knew him best, said that they knew it was a hoax and that Jesse was still alive. Now, a number of writers and historians have found information that agrees with that and have published their findings in various publications and articles, and also in at least one documentary that was shown on TV.

Living Relatives

Then recently, there has been some very interesting information that has been publicized regarding two different men who were living after the turn-of-the Century who each was believed to have been Jesse in older life. Of course, only one of them could have possibly been Jesse, not both.

But in each case, some relatives of these men have shown letters, documents, photographs, personal items, interviews, and other information that convinces them that Jesse remarried again, had a family, and that they are related to him. They both seem authentic, so one or the other could be true.

Then, what about the 101-year-old-man old man who showed up in Lawton, Oklahoma in 1947, and said that he was Jesse James and was still alive. Was he the real Jesse James? If not, then he convinced many people that he was.

The evidence is overwhelming…Jesse James was not killed by Bob Ford!

I, like most others, grew up believing that Jesse had been killed like history said it did, even thought I had always thought the story was a little strange. But in view of the latest research and evidence, especially the results of the DNA testing and the .38 caliber bullet found in the skull of the dead body, it indicates that it was someone else. And if that isn't convincing enough, take a careful look at the portrait of Jesse and of the dead body and you can see for yourself they are not the same person!

Admittedly, it may be difficult for some to reverse what they have always believed or publicly said. It could upset some traditions or position they have supported in the past and would require some changes that might be difficult, or embarrassing to do. That is understandable.

Who Would Pay For The Crime

So, if the big question came up at the end of the retrial as to who was killed and who killed him, the brothers would have a hard time convincing a court that they were innocent, and had not killed anybody—neither Jesse nor the innocent man!

Remember, in that situation, they would have been past the point of where the Governor could have been able to pardon them because his pardon had only been for killing Jesse James—not someone else.

In that case, maybe the only way to save the Fords from death would be if Jesse would suddenly appear someplace and announce that he was still alive and that he himself had killed the other person.

But would Jesse really have done that to save his friends? He might very well have done that—then immediately disappear again.

Actually, that could have really happened if the 101-year-old-man who showed up in Lawton, Oklahoma in 1948 was who he said he was: "The Real Jesse James" and that he had not been killed by Bob Ford, or any one else.

After all of those years, did we finally hear the truth--and that Jesse got away with his own murder?

The End

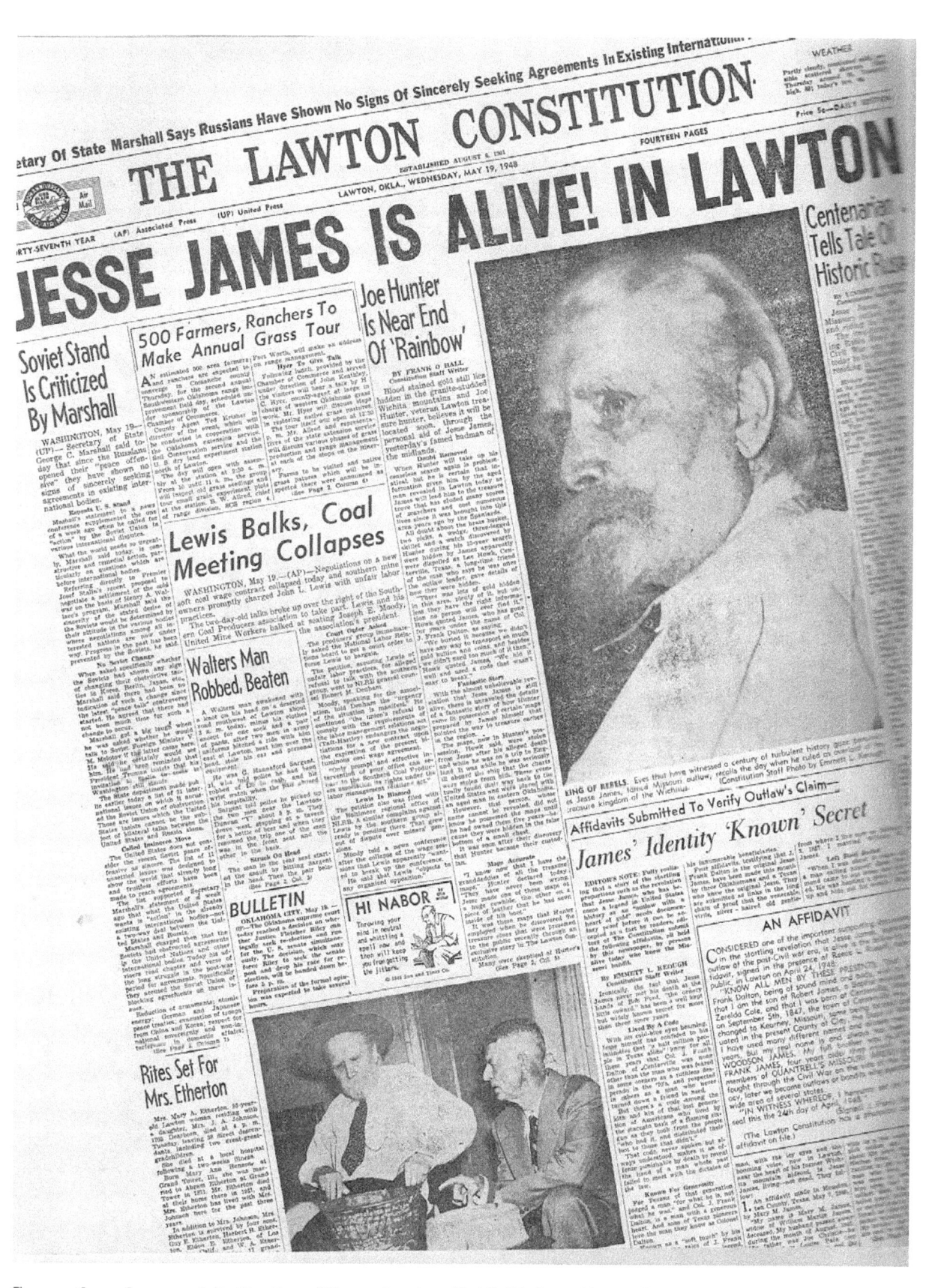

Sensational news hit the headlines in April 1947 that Jesse James is alive in Lawton, Oklahoma at the ripe old age of 100.

In a few days after the surprising headlines in April 1948, a crowd of about 20,000 people thronged in to Lawton, Oklahoma to see for themselves the old man who said that he was the real Jesse James that had supposedly been killed by Bob Ford in 1882.

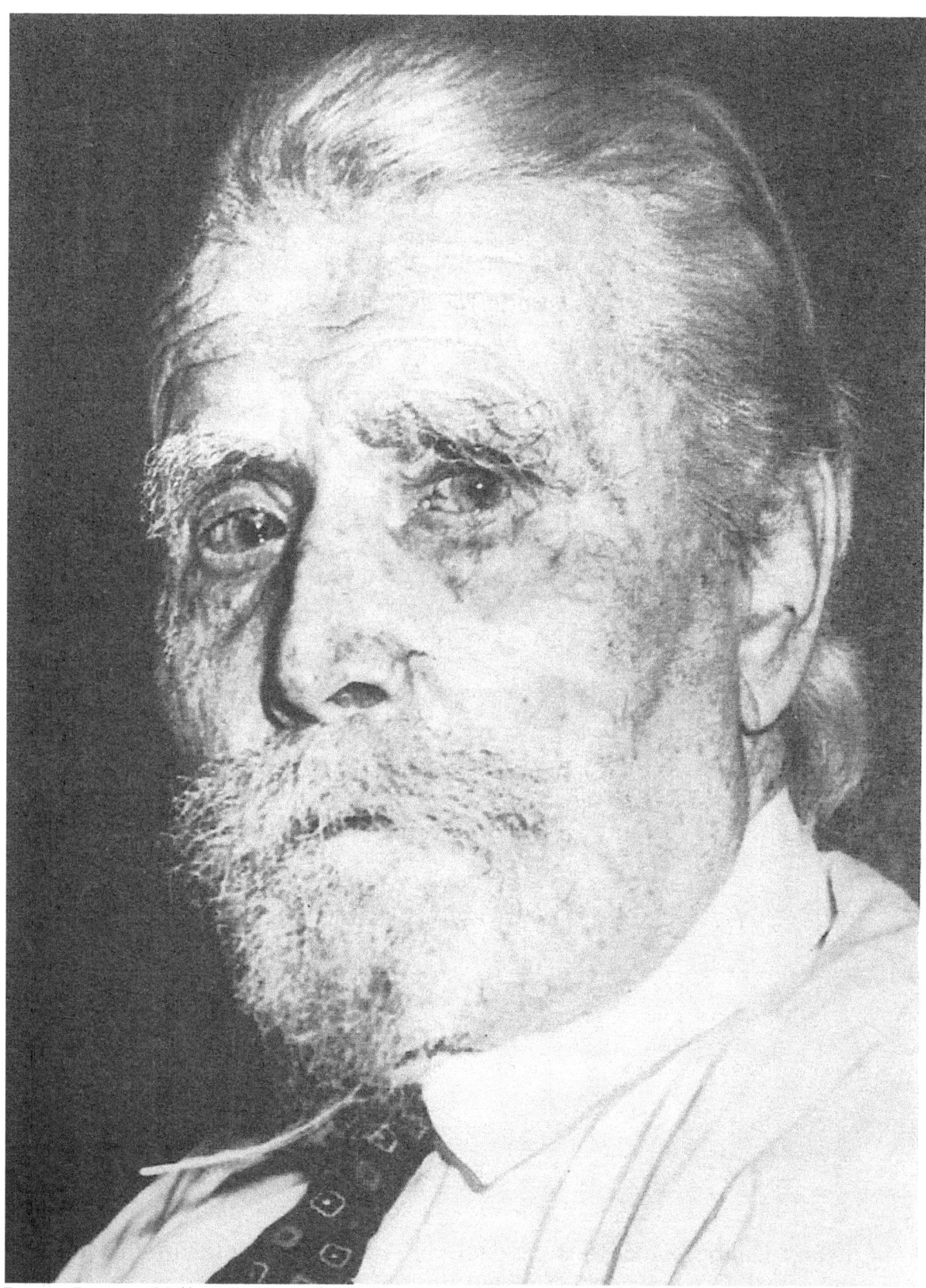

Jesse James (Alias J. Frank Dalton) at 100-years-old. Notice his piercing eyes. That was one of Jesse's noticeable characteristics that helped convince many people that it was really him.

An Affidavit

Considered one *of* the important supporting documents *in the startling* revelation that *Jesse James,* legendary outlaw of *the post-Civil war* era, *is alive is* the *following affidavit,* signed *in the* presence of Reece L. Russell, notary *public, in* Lawton on *April 24, 1948:*

"KNOW ALL MEN BY THESE PRESENTS: *That I,* J. Frank Dalton, being of sound *mind and* body, wish *to state* that *I* am tl1e son of *Robert* James, a Baptist minister, and Zerelda *Cole,* and *that I was* born at Centerville, Missouri, on ₧tember *5th, 1847.* The town of Centerville was later changed *to* Kearney, I\llissouri, same being located and situated *in the* present County of *Clay,* the State of *Missouri. I have* used many different names and *aliass*
WOODSON JAMES. My *full* brother wqs ALEXANDER FRANK *JAMES,* four years *older than* myself. We were members of *QUANTRILL'S* MISSOURI IRREGULARS *that* fought througb the *Civil* War on the side ot the Confederacy, later we became *outlaws* or *bandits* who operated *over* a *wide* area of *several states.*

"IN WITNESS WHEREOF, *I* hereunto set my hand and *seal* this *the* 24th day of *April, 1948."*

(Signed) *J.* Frank *Dalton.*

J. Frank Dalton signed this affidavit in April 1948 declaring that he was the real Jesse Woodson James, the old bandit outlaw.

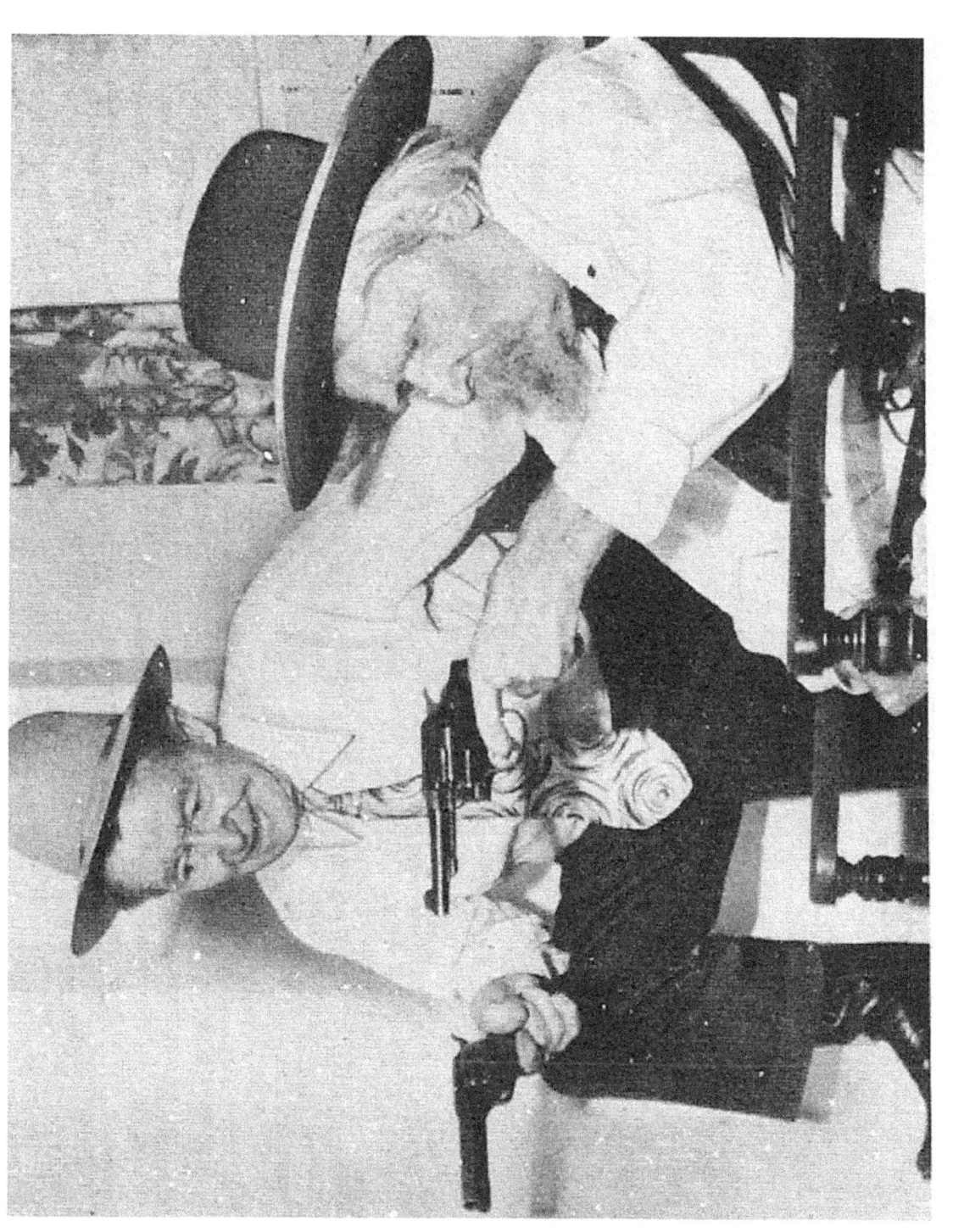

This photo shows Jesse (alias J. Frank Dalton) on the right, with the old famous Oklahoma outlaw and train robber, Al Jennings--both posing with their six-shooters. Al was brought in to identify the old man, and he said, "Boys, there isn't a bit of doubt on earth. It's him. It's Jesse James."

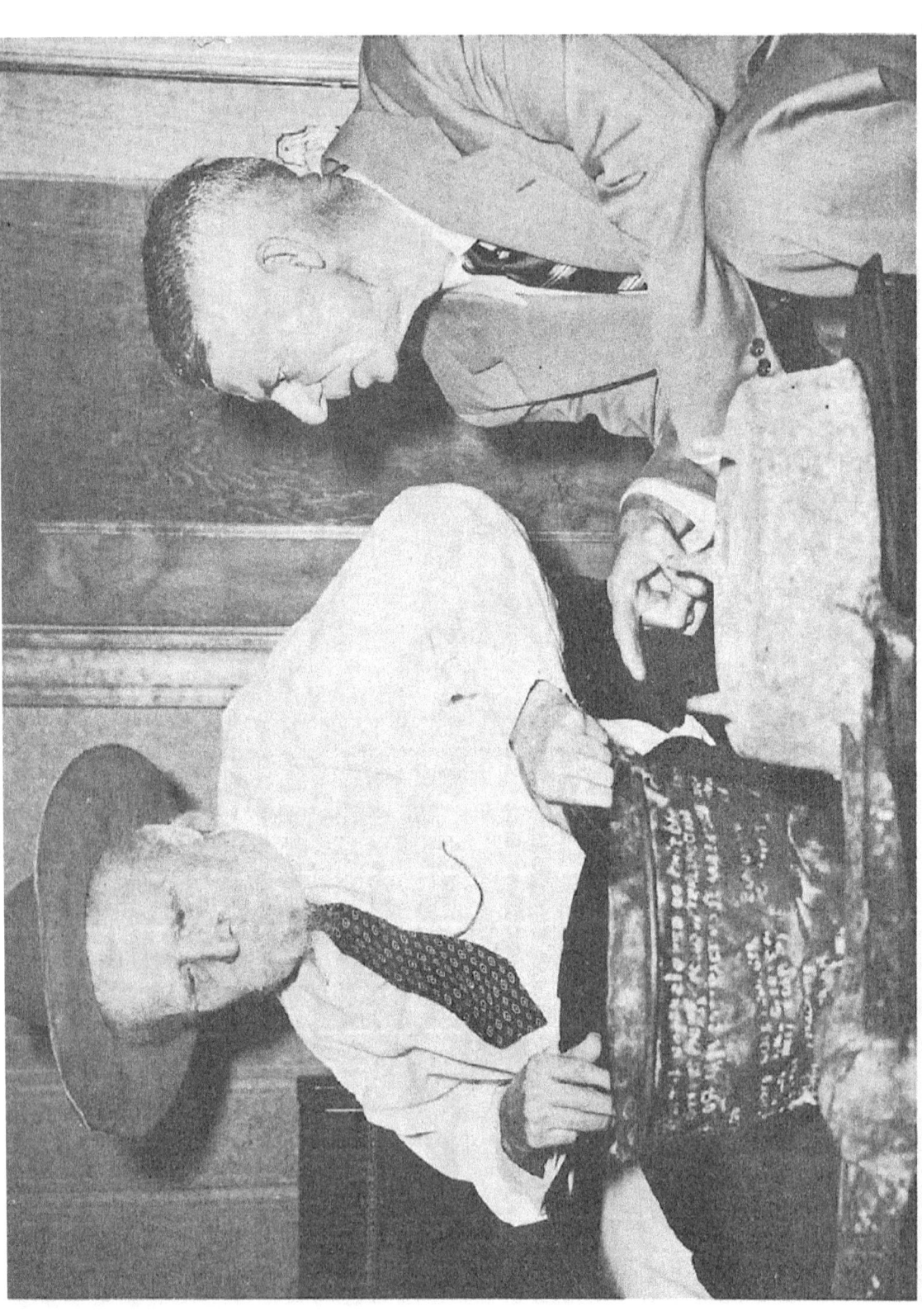

Jesse and Lawton treasure hunter, Joe Hunter, examine the old brass kettle that Jesse and his gang had buried 70 years before in the Wichita Mountains in Oklahoma. Joe had found it by following some old treasure maps. However, it had been empty and only used to inscribe a contract on by Jesse to say that the treasure the gang had just buried nearby belonged to all of them--equally. Also shown is the three-legged Dutch oven that had contained a sizable treasure that Joe had also found, and the pick heads that had been left as treasure signs.

This is the last picture of Frank James at his home in Missouri, before his natural death in 1915 at age of 72. This was after he had left Oklahoma where he had spent years looking for a treasure that the gang had once buried on property that later was owned by Mrs. Belle Hedlund. After spending a number of years looking for it, he finally gave up because the landmarks had changed. However, the treasure was found later in 1937 by Joe Hunter who used some treasure maps to locate it. That was before metal detectors were used.

About the Author Dr. Roy W. Roush

The author is one of the most recognized names in the world as an authority on the subject of Treasure Hunting and Gold Prospecting. He has also been very active in those fields and has served as a researcher and consultant for a number of organizations and individuals. He has also organizing and participating in various treasure expeditions and underwater salvage projects in the Florida Keys, Bahamas, Turks and Caicos Islands, Puerto Rico, and Mexico, as well as some locations in the United States.

Being one of the first to use a metal detector in the early 1960's, building his first one in 1962, he has searched around many of the old ghost towns, mining camps and military forts in the western part of the United States; plus looking for many of the well-known lost treasures; including: The Lost Dutchman; The 17 Tons of Gold in New Mexico; Peg Leg's Black Gold Nuggets; The Iron Door Mine; Knights of the Golden Circle Treasures; Lost Padre Mine; Black Beard's Treasure; and Treasure of Sir Frances Drake at Catalina Island, but only found a large piece of ships decking. He also discovered the remains of The Lost Arch Mine in California in 1970, however no treasure remained except for some traces of gold in the arista. His collection of many old coins, jewelry, tokens, weapons, and artifacts found at these locations is impressive.

He is a popular guest speaker on these subjects to many clubs and organizations, including: The Gold Prospectors Association; The Lost Dutchman Mining Association; The Prospectors Cub of Southern California; The Texas Council of Treasure Clubs; The Adventures' Club of Los Angeles, The California Wreck Divers Association, and The Gene Autry Museum of Western History. He is also a member of those organizations.

He has taught many courses on treasure hunting, and gold prospecting at UCLA, Los Angeles City College, The Elks Lodge in Glendale, Keene Engineering, Treasure Emporium, and has also taught Metal Detecting to some FBI agents and is a consultant to the Los Angeles Police Department on Metal Detecting,

As an expert with all kinds of metal detectors, he has won numerous National Metal Detecting Contests. His experience in gold prospecting started on his father's gold claim in Colorado in 1946. He started collecting books and articles on lost treasures while in high school and now owns one of the largest private libraries and files on treasure hunting in the world that includes thousands of books, magazines, newspaper articles, photographs, audio and video tapes.

He has traveled around most of the United States and to Europe seven times, plus four trips to the South Pacific, including New Zealand and Australia. He served with the Marines during WWII; then as a fighter pilot during the Korean War and once survived an engine explosion and crash landing of an F-80 jet fighter at Nellis AFB.

His hobbies have been flying, treasure hunting and scuba diving.

He had been the subject of many newspaper and magazine articles, TV and radio programs. Currently, he is featured on the popular Commercial DVD "Prospecting for Gold" available at most Gold Prospecting and Treasure Hunting Shops & the Internet.

www.ingramcontent.com/pod-product-compliance
Lightning Source LLC
Chambersburg PA
CBHW060316240426
43661CB00059B/2786